masterChef
AUSTRALIA

VOLUME TWO

masterChef
AUSTRALIA

VOLUME TWO

THE
COOKBOOK

HarperCollins*Publishers*
harpercollins.com.au

Contents

Winner's foreword

On 25 July 2010 approximately 5 million people across Australia watched Callum and me cook off in the MasterChef finale. It was a great day, not just for the two of us, but for all the contestants, judges and MasterChef crew who had worked so hard for so long to create something wonderful. We had shared that hard work over many months and, for me, finishing it by seeing the pride on my grandmother's face and the tears of joy in her eyes was something very special.

Aaron summed up the way all the contestants felt with his words at the end of our final Masterclass: "You enter this competition for a reason: to become Australia's next MasterChef. But along the way you get sidetracked by the people you meet, the experiences you have, the stories you can tell, and the person this competition helps you become. I just feel elated to be part of this family."

The shower of gold confetti rains down as Adam is pronounced Australia's MasterChef 2010 in front of family, friends and the Top 24.

The first half of the competition was a struggle for me, and one that took place mainly off-camera. I had quit my job as a lawyer and left my life in Japan to return home to Australia and try to follow an unconventional passion.

I was working my guts out in every challenge, cooking food that I thought the judges would like. Mud crab ravioli with tomato beurre blanc and duck breast with lavender cream and fennel confit were dishes I thought the judges wanted to see but which never made it to air because they were fairly mediocre offerings in a field of amazingly talented cooks. The judges never hated what I made, but every challenge that went by when they were blown away by someone else's dish – never mine – wore me down. I even started to question my decision to enter the MasterChef competition in the first place.

The turning point was, strangely, my three-course pizza. I knew cooking something so off-the-wall would be a risk, but I loved making it and felt it was a good reflection of the way I think about food. Unfortunately for me, the judges weren't convinced and pronounced it horrible! A reaction like that might have crushed my spirit but it seemed to have the opposite effect. I finally realised I was just happy to make food that excited me and I was willing to wear the consequences. From that point I stopped trying to make food I thought the judges would love, and started making food I knew I would love. Eventually that freedom started to pay off.

The competition was full of moments none of us will forget. Seeing Callum and Marion win in Paris on the banks of the Seine was amazing. It was their first visit to France, and years from now they might walk with their families along that promenade in front of Notre Dame and remember everything we did there.

Claire's pure happiness at winning our second signature dish challenge in front of our culinary heroes was also a pleasure to

watch. If you're lucky enough to see someone's life change in front of you, it is a humbling and precious experience.

For me personally there were hundreds of life-changing moments that will stay with me forever: winning the Qantas A380 challenge against the odds; the hard-fought cook-off with Aaron that won me an immunity pin; and meeting Michel Roux, David Chang, Heston Blumenthal and the amazing Australian chefs who shared their time and knowledge with us every week.

However, the memories I will hold most fondly in my mind are those of time spent with the other contestants, sitting on the balcony of our house after a long day of filming, and dissecting every single dish and judge's comment over a beer and a laugh. Or cooking comfort food like Jonathan's "three-hat chicken nuggets" together in the house on a day off. The fun and genuine affection we all felt for each other was evident when we filmed the final Masterclass of the series.

Food is a very personal thing. The food we make represents who we are, and on MasterChef for nearly four months we tried to show that part of ourselves to you in your homes. To all of us contestants this is not just a book of recipes; it's also a book of stories and memories. We have lived every dish in these pages and, in reading through them, we remember how privileged we are to have been a part of the competition.

I hope that as you cook your way through this book you can remember the times you shared with your family and friends watching us live through the most amazing experience of our lives.

I am proud beyond words to be Australia's MasterChef 2010, but that title would mean nothing to me without the friends I made and the journey we all travelled together.

Adam Liaw

Australia's MasterChef, 2010

Aaron HARVIE

"Serving up the perfect dish is like watching a great rock band play," says Aaron, 37, a band manager from Sydney. The beanie-wearing cook made it to the Top 7 and hit the headlines by knocking out Marion. His fish and chips didn't crunch, but he left with grace. "I look back and I'm proud. I cooked up a storm whenever I could." A series highlight was Matt Preston dropping Aaron's "disgustingly good" pasta from a great height.

Adam LIAW

Friends encouraged the Tokyo-based lawyer to apply for MasterChef, although he hadn't seen Series 1. He's been cooking for his large family since the age of eight, but food became a passion while he was at Adelaide University. "I would taste something when I was out and then make it at home. I just had people over for dinner all the time." Since becoming Australia's MasterChef, Adam, 31, has been working on his cookbook and plans for a Japanese eatery.

Adele FRAGNITO

Adele was born in Italy and emigrated to Adelaide as a child. "I was brought up in a strong Italian family and started cooking at an early age with my mum." The hairdresser thrilled George with her crostoli, but then had a sausage-roll disaster at the children's party challenge. Her younger son, Michael, has learning disabilities and, post-MasterChef, Adele has set up a scheme to teach disabled young people how to cook.

Alvin QUAH

The scientific affairs manager from Sydney loved Series 1 so much that he named a pot plant "Poh". Alvin, 35, didn't expect to make the Top 24, but came sixth. Excitable, affable and unfailingly enthusiastic (even in the face of a macaron tower), Alvin hopes to open an Asian tapas bar and release a cookbook of his and his mum's Malaysian-inspired recipes. For now, he's working on his website: cinnamonpig.com.au.

Callum HANN

At 20, the youngest competitor grew from dish-washing engineering student to runner-up MasterChef. The boy from the Barossa Valley took over the home-cooking after the death of his father a few years ago. He and Adam became firm friends and the winner says: "Callum learns so quickly, is gifted in most things he does, and will be one of the best chefs in Australia one day." He's moving to Melbourne for a three-month culinary scholarship with George Calombaris.

Carrie JOHNSTON

American Carrie, 34, moved to Sydney after finishing her Arts degree in California, and discovered a love of cooking when she married husband, Rob. Carrie went out of MasterChef in style, racing to Melbourne with Jimmy and Peter for the Stephanie Alexander pressure test. She's still determined to break into the food industry and is setting up her own catering company.

Claire WINTON BURN

For Claire, 31, cooking has always been her "happy place". After discovering a love of food with her grandmother as a child, she took a year before university to travel Europe and enrol in a cooking course. Returning to Melbourne, she suppressed her passion and went ahead with life as a lawyer. Having come third in MasterChef, she's now writing for a Melbourne newspaper and hosts small Sunday lunch functions through clairewintonburn.com.au.

Courtney ROULSTON

Courtney had worked at her local Coogee Bowling Club for more than 12 years and "lost track of time" when her upcoming 30th birthday made her re-evaluate and apply for MasterChef. After early elimination when she identified mint as "spearmint", she cooked her way to a second chance and was there for finals week. She's gaining experience as a food stylist and plans to one day open a small wine bar.

Daniel AULSEBROOK

The pork schnitzel has haunted Daniel since he left the show. After being eliminated sixth, he's spent time rectifying his lack of schnitzel knowledge. "I've made half a dozen since I arrived home and, let me tell you, they've come up a treat!" Tattooed Daniel, 32, discovered a love of cooking when he was studying classical music at Melbourne University and is now working as a wine wholesaler.

Devon HEADLAND

Someone has to go home first, and in Series 2 it was Devon, 30, the builder from Queensland's Gold Coast. He postponed his wedding to appear in MasterChef but was eliminated after the Italian restaurant challenge. "My fiancée, Cat, and I knew we had big decisions to make," he says. "But she's been behind me the whole way." Devon is now even more inspired to chase his dream. "MasterChef has lit a flame inside me. I'll get work experience in a restaurant to learn how a kitchen operates, and one day I'll open a cafc."

Dominic CORRIGAN

"Food to me is symbolic of family," says Dominic, who was inspired by his parents when it came to cooking. With four children of his own, he's used to a panel of harsh judges and became the household's main cook after being made redundant. The Black Forest cake was his MasterChef nemesis, with the complex recipe not suited to his style of family-friendly food. He's now working as CEO of a charity.

Fiona INGLIS

Home gourmand Fiona, 24, had just finished a primary teaching degree when she entered the MasterChef house. Despite fretting about her youth and lack of experience in the face of Series 2's highly skilled competitors, she put up a good performance, with her chocolate ganache tarts being Gary's "dish of the series". She's now back in her home town of Melbourne and has achieved her goal by obtaining a highly coveted primary teaching role as part of Stephanie Alexander's Kitchen Garden Program.

Jake BUJAYER

The MasterChef journey can be a roller-coaster. The cement renderer from the NSW Central Coast realised a dream in week 7 when he met culinary hero Rick Stein, then experienced a nightmare two days later with his salmon sashimi in the P&O cruise liner challenge. Eliminated on the Thai green curry taste test against Joanne, the keen fisherman has opened a weekly seafood stand at Central Coast markets.

Jimmy SEERVAI

Jimmy was sent home for "butchering" a lobster in the Rick Stein pressure test, ending his dream of making the Top 10. But then he was back, cooking a cracker of a curry to win a second chance and make it to finals week. The food ingredient researcher, 31, with the ready smile came fourth in the competition after converting chilli-hating George with his full-flavoured curries. He's keeping busy with a range of sauces, an upcoming restaurant, Jimmy's Spice Kitchen, in Sydney's Surry Hills and the arrival of his first child.

Joanne ZALM

The Sydney mother of two made Lebanese sweet doughnuts at her audition – Gary loved them so much he ate the plateful. Having grown up on a farm, Jo, 37, is no stranger to hard work and is passionate about cooking healthy food for her daughters. She faced elimination six times, finally going out in London on the roast pigeon pressure test. She's now taking on work experience as a recipe tester and food stylist.

Jonathan DADDIA

The IT consultant, 33, from Sydney was nicknamed "The Eliminator" by fellow contestants. He dispatched six competitors in pressure tests before leaving just before finals week. French food is his passion, although he obviously cooks a mean goat curry, too. The trip to London and Paris, when he cooked for his hero, Heston Blumenthal, and met Jamie Oliver, was the highlight of his MasterChef time. Jonathan is now working towards opening a French bistro or small wine bar serving food.

Kate NUGARA

Secondary school teacher Kate, 30, from Melbourne, has always challenged herself, be it with work or travel. She saw her MasterChef journey as a chance to explore her Sri Lankan heritage through cooking. Kate was the second contestant to be eliminated, going out in the all-girls pressure test on a tough Peter Gilmore chicken dish. She's gone back to teaching, but is hoping to run cultural and food tours of Melbourne and open her own food outlet.

Marion GRASBY

When Marion was eliminated in week 12, it seemed the earth might stop turning on its axis. The journalist-turned-Masters student, 27, was a popular favourite for the title but her satay sauce just didn't match up to Aaron's. Having thrilled viewers by beating chef Frank Camorra in a Melbourne laneway to gain immunity, and daringly combining mangoes with chillies and fish sauce, Marion seemed unstoppable. Back home at McLaren Vale, SA, she's working on a sauce range and writes a monthly column for MasterChef magazine.

Matthew CALDICOTT

The young third-generation accountant was rebelling against family tradition by seeking a career in the food industry. His fabulous desserts showed real culinary talent but, heartbreakingly, he was eliminated just before the trip to London. Since MasterChef, Matthew, 21, has been doing work experience at Neil Perry's Spice Temple in Sydney and will not be going back to accounting. "My parents have been very supportive and want to see me do something with this now."

Peter KRITIKIDES

"Something inside me died the moment I saw the macaron tower," says Peter, 29, who was eliminated for the second time by the towering inferno of culinary pain. Despite the tower, the chatty Melbourne lawyer loved his time on the show: "My mates nicknamed me 'Bruce McAvaney' because of the amount of running commentary I gave." He has started a small business, Urban Larder, and plans to open a providore store.

Philip **VAKOS**

Sudden death on a bouillabaisse tasting sent Philip home after the supermarket ambush challenge. The auditor, 27, from Hobart, felt he was too cautious with his dishes and, given his time again, he'd "go crazy". He is still chasing a career in the food industry and has some words of wisdom for future contestants: "Enjoy every minute in the house and the MasterChef kitchen. It really is amazing and the best thing I've ever done."

Sarah **CARMICHAEL**

Sarah, 30, has been a police detective for 10 years but put her life temporarily on hold to cook in the MasterChef kitchen. With two sons, one only seven months old, it was always going to be an emotional strain. After the Italian restaurant challenge, Sarah realised it was "the right dream, but the wrong time" and left to be with her family in Melbourne.

Sharnee **RAWSON**

Beef stroganoff might have been a family favourite in the 1970s, but it's certainly not popular with Sharnee, 21, who had never eaten it before her elimination pressure test, and now probably never will. Since making it to the MasterChef Top 10, the Brisbane law student is juggling three jobs in the food industry, working full-time at a catering company, writing healthy recipes for a personal fitness company, and food writing and reviewing restaurants for local publications. She's also finding the time to complete her law degree!

Skye **CRAIG**

Art director by day, dessert maniac by night, Skye amazed us with her unorthodox style of cooking (think lychee in a glass ball) and introduced native Australian ingredients into the MasterChef kitchen. For many of the other contestants her signature chocolate avocado mousse was a favourite dish of the series. Since being eliminated (by Jonathan The Eliminator, of course) on a spice taste test, Skye has set up a dessert company (wildsugar.com.au) and is selling her creations at markets close to her Brisbane home.

Chapter One

FIFTY BECOME 24

And their time starts now. Eight thousand entrants become 50 hopefuls who battle for 24 places. The journey begins with a hot barbecue and a crisp Donna Hay pavlova. They judge signature dishes, master beef Wellington and lift the lid on the first mystery box. After all that, some still have to roll gnocchi for Matt Moran and poach Neil Perry's snapper.

Devon's BEEF CARPACCIO WITH GINGER CHILLI DRESSING

Devon isn't scared of new flavours. He has travelled widely through Asia and makes a point of sampling unusual foods. So it made sense that his audition beef carpaccio wasn't going to be a run-of-the-mill traditional Italian sliced beef with creamy dressing. The judges took one taste of this Asian-inspired dish and he was into the Top 50.

250g good-quality beef fillet
Peanut oil, to deep-fry
1 potato, peeled
25g baby rocket leaves
1 lime, juiced
25g parmesan, shaved

DRESSING
2 tbs extra virgin olive oil
2 tbs balsamic vinegar
2 tbs soy sauce
2cm piece ginger, peeled, grated

1 bird's-eye chilli, finely chopped
2 red eschalots, finely chopped
1 tbs finely chopped chives

1 Wrap the beef tightly in plastic wrap and freeze for 3 hours or until firm but not frozen through.
2 To make the dressing, whisk together oil, vinegar and soy sauce. Add ginger, chilli, eschalots and chives and mix together.
3 Fill a deep-fryer or large saucepan one-third full with peanut oil and heat over medium heat to 180°C (or until a cube of bread turns golden in 10 seconds). Using a potato peeler, peel thin ribbons from the potato. Pat dry with paper towel. Working in batches, fry potato ribbons for 4 minutes or until golden and crisp. Lift out with a slotted spoon and drain on paper towel. Season with salt.
4 Unwrap the beef. Using a large, very sharp knife, cut the beef across the grain into paper-thin slices. Arrange on plates, overlapping slightly. Drizzle with the dressing. Toss the rocket with lime juice and pile over carpaccio with the crisp potato ribbons and parmesan.

SEMI-FREEZING the beef beforehand makes it much easier to slice thinly. Make sure you let the sliced beef come back to room temperature before serving so the full flavour comes through.

Jake's SALMON TASTING PLATE

Jake loves to cook, but for him the real thrill is in the catch: "I'm pretty obsessed with fishing, from snapper to kingfish. I like to get out and catch something at least once a week. I'd say I'm addicted to seafood." When the judges tasted this audition dish of salmon tartare and gravlax, they realised that seafood is not only his addiction but also his great talent.

500g coarse sea salt
400g white sugar
1 bunch dill, chopped
1 side of salmon, pin-boned
¼ cup crème fraîche
1 cup watercress leaves

2cm piece fresh horseradish,
    very finely grated
2 tsp salmon roe˚
350g sashimi-grade salmon˚
½ cup mayonnaise
2 tsp wasabi paste

¼ cup peeled, seeded, diced
    Lebanese cucumber
¼ cup diced avocado flesh
2 tsp tobiko (flying fish roe)˚
Toasted sourdough bread,
    to serve

1 To make gravlax, mix together the salt, sugar and dill. Spread half the mixture onto a non-reactive tray and lay the salmon fillet on top. Cover with the remaining salt mixture. Cover tightly with plastic wrap and refrigerate for 24 hours to cure the salmon.

2 Drain moisture from the cured salmon and wipe clean of salt mixture. Using a thin sharp knife, thinly slice the salmon. Cut 150g of the sliced salmon into fine dice and combine with the crème fraîche, watercress and horseradish. Pile neatly onto a platter and top with salmon roe.

3 Cut 100g from the sashimi salmon and cut into 1cm dice. Combine with the mayonnaise, wasabi, cucumber and avocado. Place in a neat pile on the platter and top with the tobiko.

4 Cut the remaining 250g sashimi salmon into 1cm-thick slices. Add the sashimi slices and cured salmon slices to the platter and serve with toasted sourdough.

SALMON ROE, SASHIMI-GRADE SALMON AND TOBIKO are all available from good fishmongers.

As the fisherman and seafood expert of series 2, Jake was "absolutely stoked" to meet his idol, Rick Stein. Unfortunately, the occasion was a pressure test but Jake's seafood platter was good enough to see him through.

Serves **4**
Preparation **35 minutes**
Cooking **35 minutes**

Peter's WHITING INVOLTINI & CAPONATA

Peter made this Sicilian dish for his first audition. "With its big, bold flavours, this represents everything I love about food. Cooking in front of cameras was utterly nerve-wracking, but George and Gary announced I was into the Top 50, so this dish changed my life!"

CAPONATA

80ml (1/3 cup) balsamic vinegar
1 tbs sugar
2 tbs olive oil
1 onion, diced
1 clove garlic, finely sliced
1 eggplant, diced
1 zucchini, diced
1 stalk celery, diced
1 red capsicum, roasted, peeled, sliced
55g (1/3 cup) pitted kalamata olives

2 tbs capers
2 tbs raisins
160ml (2/3 cup) tomato passata
2 tbs shredded parsley or oregano

INVOLTINI

40g (1/4 cup) currants
80ml (1/3 cup) olive oil
70g (1 cup) fresh sourdough breadcrumbs
1 onion, finely diced
40g (1/4 cup) pine nuts, roasted
1/4 cup finely chopped parsley

1/2 lemon, zested, juiced
1/2 orange, juiced
4 whiting fillets
8 fresh bay leaves

DRESSING

1 tbs dried oregano
1 clove garlic, finely chopped
125ml (1/2 cup) extra virgin olive oil
1/2 lemon, juiced
1 tbs finely chopped parsley

1 To make caponata, combine balsamic vinegar and sugar in a small saucepan and simmer gently until thickened and slightly reduced. Heat the oil in a frying pan and fry onion and garlic until softened. Add eggplant, zucchini and celery and cook over medium heat for 8–10 minutes or until softened (but not stewed). Remove from heat and gently stir in roasted capsicum, olives, capers, raisins and the reduced balsamic vinegar. Add passata and stir over low heat until caponata is warmed through. Add parsley or oregano and season with salt and black pepper.

2 To make involtini, preheat oven to 170°C. Put currants in a small bowl with 60ml (1/4 cup) boiling water and leave for 10 minutes until plump. Heat 60ml (1/4 cup) of the olive oil in a frying pan and gently fry the breadcrumbs until golden. Set breadcrumbs aside to cool and wipe out pan.

3 Heat remaining olive oil in clean frying pan and gently fry the onion over medium heat for 5 minutes until translucent. Add the breadcrumbs, drained currants, pine nuts, parsley, lemon zest and lemon and orange juices. Season well and set aside to cool.

4 Put the whiting skin-side down between 2 sheets of baking paper. Gently pound until the fillets are of even thickness. With tail end of the fish closest to you, place 1 heaped tbs of breadcrumb mixture on the fillet and roll up away from you. Secure with a toothpick and attach a bay leaf to each side of the fish. Repeat with rest of fillets. Gently press extra stuffing into the top of each involtini to make a generous mound. Place on an oiled oven tray and bake for 10 minutes or until cooked through.

5 To make dressing, pound oregano, garlic and a pinch of salt to a paste with a mortar and pestle, then slowly add oil and lemon juice, stirring continuously. Season with salt and pepper and add parsley.

6 Serve the involtini drizzled with the dressing, with the caponata on the side.

Claire's ASIAN CHICKEN COOKED TWO WAYS

"This is your chance to cook the best barbecue of your life," said George, and Claire took the instruction to heart. For the barbecue challenge Matt wanted imaginative dishes with vibrant flavours: "If you can't cook with fire you have no place in this competition." Claire certainly staked her place with this perfect balance of sweet and sour flavours.

1 x 1.6kg chicken, wings
  separated, plus 6 extra wings
1 onion, halved
2 cloves garlic, peeled
2 limes, zested
1 tbs black peppercorns
60ml (¼ cup) soy sauce
2 tbs honey

4 spring onions, white part only,
  finely chopped
3 cloves garlic, finely chopped,
  plus extra, sliced, to serve
2 large red chillies, chopped
1 Lebanese cucumber
⅓ cup Vietnamese mint leaves
½ cup Thai basil leaves

1 cup coriander leaves
80ml (⅓ cup) lime juice
2 tbs fish sauce
1½ tbs grated palm sugar
½ pineapple, thinly sliced
  crosswise

1 Place the whole chicken (without wings) in a large saucepan with the onion, whole garlic cloves, half the lime zest, and the peppercorns. Cover with water and bring slowly to the boil. Reduce the heat to low–medium and simmer, covered, for 45 minutes or until the chicken juices run clear when the thigh is pierced. Remove chicken from the pan and leave for 15 minutes until cool enough to handle. Pull the meat from the chicken and shred, discarding skin. Set aside.

2 Meanwhile, combine the soy sauce, honey, remaining lime zest, spring onions, chopped garlic and half the chillies. Pour over the 8 chicken wings in a shallow, non-reactive dish and marinate in the fridge for 45 minutes.

3 Using a vegetable peeler, peel the cucumber into long ribbons. Combine with the herbs, the remaining chopped chilli and the shredded chicken.

4 To make the dressing, mix together the lime juice, fish sauce and palm sugar. Toss through the salad.

5 Preheat a barbecue or chargrill to low–medium. Cook the wings for 5 minutes each side or until browned and cooked. Cook the pineapple for 2 minutes each side or until slightly caramelised.

6 To serve, arrange the pineapple on plates and top with the chicken salad and chicken wings. Sprinkle with sliced red chilli.

USE A VEGETABLE PEELER
to slice the cucumber into thin
ribbons. Try to avoid the seeds.

Sarah's MANGO, RASPBERRY & TOFFEED MACADAMIA PAVLOVA

The Donna Hay pavlova challenge was a Top 50 elimination test: the pavlova had to match Donna's, with its beautiful, high, crisp crust and marshmallow inside. Sarah came through in style with this fruity, toffeed topping. Matt Preston was impressed: "Crust, marshmallow, topping, texture, balance of flavours, and it looks dead-set delicious. Six out of six."

PAVLOVA

4 egg whites
220g (1 cup) caster sugar
2 tbs cornflour, sifted
2 tsp white vinegar

TOPPING

300ml thickened cream
1 tsp vanilla bean paste
1 large mango
50g macadamias, chopped

1½ tbs brown sugar
250g raspberries
1 tbs icing sugar

1 To make pavlova, preheat oven to 150°C. Use an electric mixer to whisk the egg whites to stiff peaks, then gradually add the sugar, whisking until thick and glossy. Add the cornflour and vinegar, and whisk. Shape the mixture into an 18cm round on an oven tray lined with baking paper.

2 Place in the oven, reduce temperature to 120°C and bake for 1 hour 20 minutes. Turn off the oven and leave the pavlova to cool completely inside.

3 To make topping, use an electric mixer to whisk the cream and vanilla paste to soft peaks. Cut cheeks from the mango and, using a small sharp knife, cut skin away from flesh, removing as little flesh as possible. Lay cheeks flat-side up on an oven tray. Sprinkle with macadamias and brown sugar.

4 Cook the mango cheeks under a medium–hot grill, not too close to the heat or the nuts will burn, for 3 minutes or until the sugar has melted and caramelised. Cool, then cut into slices.

5 Spread the pavlova with the cream. Arrange the raspberries and mango over the cream. Dust with icing sugar to serve.

Sarah kept her great sense of humour even when she knocked the top off her pavlova as she took it out of the oven. The onlookers on the mezzanine gasped and she laughed, "I've got another one. It's OK".

Serves **6**
Preparation **40 minutes**
+ 2 hours refrigeration
Cooking **55 minutes**

Adele's HERBED GOAT'S CHEESE & EGGPLANT WITH CURRANT & PINE NUT DRESSING

"I really enjoyed the signature dish challenge because we all cooked from the heart," said Adele. She loves cooking with creamy goat's cheese and this dish evolved around the kitchen table with her family. "I would experiment with goat's cheese and fresh seasonal vegetables and my elder son, Matthew, who's a great cook, chose this one as the best. In fact, he gave it 10 out of 10, so I felt very confident cooking it on the show."

3 eggplants

Salt, to sprinkle

3 ripe roma tomatoes, halved lengthwise, seeded

4 red capsicums, seeded, cut into flat pieces

300g soft goat's cheese

180g fresh ricotta

1 clove garlic, crushed

1/3 cup chopped basil

2 tbs chopped thyme

1 cup mustard cress*

Crusty Italian-style bread, to serve

CURRANT & PINE NUT DRESSING

180ml (3/4 cup) olive oil

60ml (1/4 cup) red wine vinegar

1 tbs honey

55g (1/3 cup) currants

50g (1/3 cup) pine nuts, toasted

1 Preheat oven to 180°C. Cut the eggplants lengthwise into 5mm slices, lay out in a single layer and sprinkle generously with salt. Leave for 30 minutes. Rinse and pat dry with paper towels.

2 Arrange the tomatoes cut-side up in an ovenproof dish and bake for 30 minutes or until soft.

3 Meanwhile, preheat a chargrill. Lightly oil the eggplant slices and cook on the chargrill for 5 minutes each side or until browned and tender. Set aside to cool. Meanwhile, cook the capsicums on a foil-lined tray under a hot grill until the skin has blackened and blistered. Place into a plastic bag for 10 minutes to cool. Peel off the skins.

4 Combine the goat's cheese, ricotta, garlic, basil and thyme. Season with salt and pepper and mix well.

5 Lightly oil 6 ring moulds* 7cm in diameter and 5cm high. Line the bases and sides with eggplant. Spread about 1 tbs of the cheese mixture into each base, then add a tomato half. Add another layer of cheese, some capsicum, more cheese, then a layer of eggplant on top. Press down firmly and cover with plastic wrap. Refrigerate for 2 hours, or until firm.

6 To make dressing, whisk the oil, vinegar and honey together until well combined, then add the currants and pine nuts. Place the eggplant moulds on plates and slide the rings up and off. Sprinkle the cress around the plate. Drizzle with the dressing and serve with bread.

USE ANY SMALL HERB leaves in place of mustard cress. MOULDS are available from specialist kitchenware shops.

"They loved it! They just kept coming back for more until they polished off the plate." Adele

Daniel's CHICKEN WITH DATES & HONEY

As far as Daniel was concerned he didn't really have a signature dish. But whenever his friends and family come over they want to eat his chicken tagine... Sounds like a great signature dish then. For Daniel, cooking is about "the social side. It's about having mates around for dinner and having a laugh". He also has the skills to go with the sociability, getting into the Top 24 with a perfect score in the mise en place preparation challenge.

3 tsp cumin seeds
3 tsp coriander seeds
2 tsp fennel seeds
12 cardamom pods, seeds removed
1 tsp black peppercorns
1/2 tsp sea salt
80ml (1/3 cup) olive oil
2 onions, finely diced

2 cloves garlic, crushed
4cm piece ginger, finely grated
2 long red chillies, seeded, finely chopped
1/2 tsp ground ginger
1 tsp ground turmeric
2 cinnamon quills
1kg chicken thigh fillets, each cut into 3 pieces

500ml (2 cups) chicken stock
10 fresh dates, pitted, chopped
80ml (1/3 cup) honey
35g (1/4 cup) slivered almonds, lightly roasted
1/3 cup coriander leaves, chopped
Couscous, to serve

1 Using a mortar and pestle, finely grind the cumin, coriander, fennel and cardamom seeds with the peppercorns and salt. Pass through a fine sieve.
2 Heat the olive oil in a flameproof tagine, casserole or heavy-based saucepan over low heat. Add the onions and cook for 3 minutes, then stir in the garlic, ginger and chillies and cook for 5 minutes or until soft. Add the spice mixture, ground ginger, turmeric and cinnamon quills. Cook over low heat for 2 minutes until fragrant.
3 Increase the heat to medium–high and add the chicken. Cook for 5 minutes each side, turning occasionally, or until light golden. Pour in the stock. Reduce the heat to low, cover and simmer for 50 minutes. Add the dates and honey and cook, uncovered, for a further 10 minutes. Remove the chicken from the pan with a slotted spoon.
4 Increase the heat to medium–high and cook for 5 minutes or until the liquid has reduced. Return the chicken to the pan and add the almonds and coriander. Serve the tagine with couscous.

TO ROAST SLIVERED ALMONDS, preheat the oven to 180°C. Spread the almonds onto an oven tray and roast for 3 minutes or until fragrant and golden.

Jimmy's CRISPY OKRA & CHILLI MUD CRAB CURRY WITH ATTA PARATHA

"Wow, that's hot! Let's hope the girls can handle a bit of heat," said Gary, when he took his first mouthful of Jimmy's signature dish. "There's a lot of flavour going on there. I love that, but wow, it's hot."

George, who famously doesn't enjoy chilli, was totally convinced. "I'd sit there with a big towel around my neck and devour all of it."

This crispy okra and chilli mud crab curry is a completely unique Jimmy-blend of flavours. "It's a product of growing up in a spice shop. We had Indian, Sri Lankan, Malaysian, Thai, Afghani customers... They all liked to tell me stories of their countries, but I was too young to travel, so the world came to the shop instead. They would choose spices for their traditional dishes and, as a child, I picked out and remembered the ingredients that sounded best to me. I was so proud when the judges chose this curry as dish of the day because it's a true mixture of world flavours."

CORIANDER ROOTS are widely used in Asian cookery, especially Thai dishes, reflecting the cosmopolitan nature of Jimmy's curry. They have as much flavour as the leaves, if not more. Wash well before use.

"I just put it all in the pot, crossed my fingers and wished for the best."

Jimmy's CRISPY OKRA & CHILLI CRAB CURRY WITH ATTA PARATHA

Serves **6**
Preparation **3 hours**
Cooking **1 hour 50 minutes**

1 fresh coconut
1 tbs sunflower oil
1½ tsp ground turmeric
1 tbs garam masala
5 star anise
½ tsp amchur powder*
2 bay leaves
1 stem cassia bark
65g (¼ cup) palm sugar
2 tbs soy sauce
1 tsp fish sauce
5 fresh curry leaves
½ tsp tamarind paste
2 tsp sea salt
4 large tomatoes, puréed
500ml (2 cups) fish stock
600ml coconut milk
3 large mud crabs, sedated for
    2 hours beforehand*

60ml (¼ cup) peanut oil
600g okra,* cut into 1cm pieces
100g coriander leaves
2 tsp finely chopped coriander
    roots
1 lemon, halved

PARATHA
675g (4½ cups) atta flour
1 tsp salt
375ml (1½ cups) milk
90g butter, melted
30g ghee*
Vegetable oil, for brushing
3 tsp nigella seeds

CURRY PASTE
1 large onion, roughly chopped
4 cloves garlic
½ stalk lemongrass, white part
    only, roughly chopped

2 tsp chopped coriander roots
1.5cm piece fresh turmeric,
    roughly chopped
3 kaffir lime leaves
3 bird's-eye chillies, chopped
2 long green chillies, chopped
5cm piece fresh ginger, chopped
3cm piece fresh galangal,
    chopped
4 fresh curry leaves
3 whole dried Kashmiri chillies

GROUND SPICE MIXTURE
1 tsp black peppercorns
10g (¼ cup) coriander seeds
2 tbs cumin seeds
½ tsp sesame seeds

1 **To make paratha,** mix flour and salt in a large bowl and make a well in the centre. Heat milk, butter and ghee in a small saucepan until the butter and ghee have just melted. Add to the flour and mix with a wooden spoon, then with your hands to form a soft dough. Add a little more milk, if necessary. Turn out onto a lightly floured surface and knead for 7–10 minutes or until smooth and elastic. Cover with plastic wrap and set aside for 1 hour to rest.

2 **To prepare coconut,** preheat oven to 200°C. Pierce a skewer through the eyes of coconut and drain out the liquid. Bake the coconut for 20 minutes, then cool. Tap around the middle of the coconut with a hammer until it cracks open. Prise flesh from shell with a butter knife. Peel off skin, then coarsely grate the flesh. You need 150g grated coconut for this recipe. Pat dry with paper towel.

3 **To make curry paste,** mix all ingredients in a food processor to a smooth paste, adding 1–2 tbs warm water if necessary.

4 **To make ground spice mixture,** place all ingredients in a dry frying pan and cook over low–medium heat for 5 minutes, stirring occasionally, until roasted and fragrant. Cool, then grind in a spice grinder or using a mortar and pestle. Set aside.

5 Put the grated coconut in a dry frying pan and stir over medium heat for 8–10 minutes or until golden

Ensuring that you kill the crab humanely also gives the crabmeat better flavour. You can ask your fishmonger to do it for you, if necessary.

brown. Grind as finely as possible in a spice grinder or using a mortar and pestle and set aside.

6 Heat the sunflower oil in a large heavy-based saucepan over medium heat. Add 125ml (½ cup) of the curry paste and cook, stirring, for 2–3 minutes or until starting to brown. Add the ground turmeric, garam masala, star anise, amchur powder, bay leaves, cassia bark and ground spice mixture. Cook, stirring, for 5 minutes over low–medium heat.

• Stir in palm sugar, soy and fish sauces, curry leaves, tamarind and salt. Cook, stirring, for a further 3 minutes. Add the puréed tomatoes and grated coconut and cook for 2 minutes. Stir in fish stock and coconut milk. Reduce heat to low and simmer for 15 minutes or until thickened.

7 **To prepare the crabs,** using a large knife or cleaver, cut the crabs into quarters **(PIC 1)**. Remove the gills **(PIC 2)**, separate the claws from the body and crack the claws **(PIC 3)** so they absorb the sauce during cooking. Add crab to sauce, cover pan and cook for 10 minutes or until crab changes colour.

8 Divide paratha dough into 12 portions and roll each portion out to a 20cm round about 2mm thick. Brush with the oil and sprinkle with nigella seeds. Roll with rolling pin to press the seeds into dough.

• Heat a large non-stick frying pan or barbecue plate over medium heat and cook paratha for 2 minutes on each side or until browned and blistered. Cover with foil and keep warm.

9 Heat peanut oil in a frying pan and cook okra over medium heat for 5 minutes or until golden brown and crisp. Drain on paper towel. Season with black pepper.

10 Stir coriander leaves and roots into curry, spoon into bowls, squeeze lemon juice over the top and sprinkle with okra. Serve with paratha.

AMCHUR POWDER is ground dried green mango and is available from Herbie's Spices in Sydney or by mail order (herbies.com.au). PUT THE CRABS in your freezer for 2 hours before cooking to sedate them humanely. OKRA is a small pod-style vegetable sometimes known as ladyfingers and available from greengrocers. GHEE is clarified butter used in Indian cooking. It is available in tubs from most supermarkets. PARATHA can be made up to 2 hours ahead. Wrap tightly in foil to prevent drying out and reheat in a low oven for 15–20 minutes. SOME CURRY PASTE will be left over. Keep, covered, in the fridge for up to 1 week or freeze for up to 1 month.

Jonathan's SADDLE OF LAMB WITH MOROCCAN SPICED DATES

Jonathan's heritage is Moroccan and the flavours of the tagine play a huge role in his cooking style. He came one step closer to the Top 24 when his classic French-style saddle of lamb signature dish excelled in the eyes of the women judges. Alvin thought the critique process of the women judging the men and vice versa was "a lot like speed dating".

1 x 1.2kg saddle of lamb, boned
200g caul fat
1 clove garlic, halved
1 tbs olive oil
2 cloves garlic, bruised
500ml (2 cups) lamb or
   veal stock
4 sprigs thyme

50g cold butter, chopped
500g baby spinach
STUFFING
100g fresh dates, pitted
40g slivered almonds
2 tsp lemon juice
1 tsp ground ginger
1 tsp ground cinnamon

½ tsp ground black pepper
½ tsp ground cumin
PARSNIP PUREE
6 parsnips (1.2 kg), peeled
500ml (2 cups) milk
1 bouquet garni
125ml (½ cup) pouring cream

1 Preheat oven to 200°C. Trim skin and excess fat from lamb and remove fillets if still attached. Score fat in a lattice pattern. Place the lamb onto the caul fat. Rub with the cut garlic and season with salt and freshly ground black pepper.

2 To make stuffing, combine all the ingredients in a small food processor and process to a paste. Spread over the lamb and roll the belly flaps over to enclose. Wrap the lamb neatly in the caul fat, roll and tie with kitchen string at 3cm intervals.

3 Heat 1 tbs oil in a large ovenproof frying pan over medium–high heat. Add the lamb and brown all over. Drain excess fat from the pan, then transfer pan to the oven and roast lamb for 30 minutes for medium–rare. Cover loosely with foil and leave to rest for 20 minutes.

4 To make parsnip purée, cut the parsnips into quarters lengthwise and remove the cores. Chop the parsnips and put in a saucepan with the milk and bouquet garni. Bring to the boil, reduce the heat to medium and cook for 8 minutes or until tender. Drain, discarding bouquet garni, then purée in a food processor until smooth. Add the cream, process until combined and season to taste. Keep warm.

5 Transfer the lamb to a board. Add the bruised garlic to the frying pan and cook over medium heat for 2 minutes, until just beginning to soften. Add the stock and thyme, bring to the boil and cook over medium–high heat for 7 minutes or until reduced by one-third. Strain into a small saucepan, place over low-medium heat and whisk in the butter a little at a time until smooth and glossy.

6 Cook spinach in boiling water for 30 seconds until wilted. Drain, squeeze out water and season well.

7 Cut the lamb into thick slices. Place spinach on plates, top with lamb and spoon parsnip purée on the side. Serve drizzled with the sauce.

CAUL FAT is a thin lacy 'net' of fat that is used to keep meat moist during the cooking process and help it keep its shape. You will need to order caul fat in advance from your butcher.

Serves **6**
Preparation **40 minutes**
Cooking **30 minutes**

Claire's SPICED LAMB RACK WITH HERBED COUSCOUS & POMEGRANATE DRESSING

The women's signature dishes were to be judged by the men. Claire decided: "It's a cliché, but I'm going to feed the men meat. I want to make them come back for more." "Knockout!" was one verdict on her spicy lamb, with its punchy harissa and pomegranate flavours.

2 lamb racks, frenched (9 cutlets
each rack)
1 pomegranate, seeds extracted

HARISSA POMEGRANATE PASTE
2 tsp coriander seeds
2 tsp cumin seeds
8 long red chillies, seeded,
chopped
2 tsp ground smoked paprika
4 cloves garlic, chopped

2 tbs tomato paste
1 tsp white wine vinegar
80ml (1/3 cup) olive oil
60ml (1/4 cup) pomegranate
molasses*
2 tbs brown sugar
1 lemon, zested

YOGHURT DRESSING
200g (3/4 cup) Greek yoghurt
1 tbs lemon juice

HERBED COUSCOUS
300g couscous
100ml olive oil
450ml boiling chicken stock
110g (1 cup) slivered pistachios,
lightly roasted*
1/2 cup chopped coriander leaves
3/4 cup chopped mint leaves

1. Preheat oven to 220°C. To make harissa, toast the coriander and cumin seeds in a dry frying pan over medium heat for 1 minute, tossing regularly, or until fragrant. Cool, then, using a mortar and pestle, grind to a powder. Combine in a small food processor with the chillies, paprika, garlic, tomato paste and vinegar. Add a good pinch of salt and process to a paste. With the motor running, gradually add the oil in a thin stream. Combine the harissa with the pomegranate molasses, sugar and lemon zest.

2. Score the lamb fat lightly, without cutting through to the meat. Cover the meat with 1/2 cup of the harissa pomegranate paste.* Place on a rack in a roasting pan and pour 250ml (1 cup) water into the pan. Roast for 25 minutes for rare, then set aside in a warm place to rest for 10 minutes.

3. To make yoghurt dressing, whisk together the yoghurt and lemon juice. Thin with a little water to a drizzling consistency. Season with salt and pepper.

4. To make herbed couscous, place the couscous in a large bowl and drizzle with the olive oil. Rub with your fingers to coat the grains with oil. Add the stock and stir briefly, then cover tightly with foil or a plate and leave for 5 minutes or until the stock has been absorbed. Season with salt, fluff the grains with a fork and cool slightly. Mix in the pistachios and herbs.

5. Carve the lamb into cutlets and serve on a bed of herbed couscous, drizzled with the yoghurt dressing. Scatter the pomegranate seeds around the plate.

POMEGRANATE MOLASSES can be found in delis and Middle Eastern grocers. TO ROAST SLIVERED PISTACHIOS, preheat the oven to 180°C. Spread the pistachios on an oven tray and roast for 3 minutes or until fragrant and golden. Cool. LEFTOVER HARISSA POMEGRANATE PASTE will keep in the fridge for up to 1 week. Use in dressings, or add to stir-fries or stews for a flavour boost.

Serves **4**
Preparation **1 hour**
Cooking **40 minutes**

Skye's CHOCOLATE AVOCADO MOUSSE WITH HIBISCUS & NATIVE PLUM COULIS

Skye had a moment of self-doubt with her signature dish: "Here I am throwing masses of bright green avocados into the blender and for just a moment I thought 'are these guys actually going to like this?' Thank goodness this recipe had been 'bloke-tested' before I got started in the MasterChef kitchen. Jonathan told me it was one of the best things he had ever tasted. That's a compliment I will never forget."

4 wild hibiscus flowers in syrup,*
   drained
70g (¹/₂ cup) raw macadamia
   nuts
1 tbs light agave nectar* (or sugar
   syrup)

MOUSSE

100g dark chocolate (70% cocoa
   solids)
4 avocados, peeled, chopped
2 tsp coconut oil
250ml (1 cup) light agave nectar
60g (¹/₂ cup) cacao powder*

HIBISCUS AND PLUM COULIS

120g Davidson plums,* halved,
   stones removed
4 wild hibiscus flowers in syrup,
   drained
125ml (¹/₂ cup) light agave nectar

1 Place 4 hibiscus flowers upside-down on a plate and freeze for 30 minutes, so they will sit upright when served. Pulse macadamia nuts and agave nectar in a food processor until roughly chopped, then take out half and set aside. Pulse the remainder until a smooth paste forms, then remove from processor and combine with the roughly chopped nuts. Set aside.

2 To make the mousse, pulse dark chocolate into small pieces in a food processor and set aside. Combine avocado flesh, coconut oil, agave nectar and cacao in a food processor and mix until smooth and creamy. Fold in chopped chocolate.

3 Spoon macadamias into four 200ml glasses and smooth with back of spoon. Spoon mousse into the glasses and smooth again. Cover with plastic wrap and freeze for 1 hour, or until semi-frozen.*

4 To make hibiscus and plum coulis, purée plums and hibiscus flowers in a blender. Add agave nectar and 60ml (¹/₄ cup) water, mix briefly and pour into a saucepan. Bring to the boil, reduce heat to low and simmer for 30 minutes. Taste and add more agave nectar if you would like it sweeter. Strain through a sieve to make a smooth coulis.

5 Pour a little coulis over the mousse and place a wild hibiscus flower on top or serve coulis separately.

HIBISCUS FLOWERS in syrup are available from delis, specialist food shops and some health food shops, or try nicholsonfinefoods.com.au. AGAVE NECTAR is a natural sweetener, available from health food shops. You could use sugar syrup instead. RAW CACAO is a nutritious alternative to cocoa powder. It is available from health food shops. DAVIDSON PLUMS are Australian native plum-like fruit with dark purple skins and vibrant dark-red flesh. They are available from native food specialists (try playingwithfire.com.au). If you can't find Davidson plums, use frozen raspberries instead. YOU CAN MAKE the mousse in advance and keep in the freezer in glasses. Soften in the fridge for 30 minutes before adding coulis and wild hibiscus flower. This dessert is best served semi-frozen.

40 MasterChef *fifty become 24*

"This is definitely my signature, 100 per cent. This is me on a plate." Skye

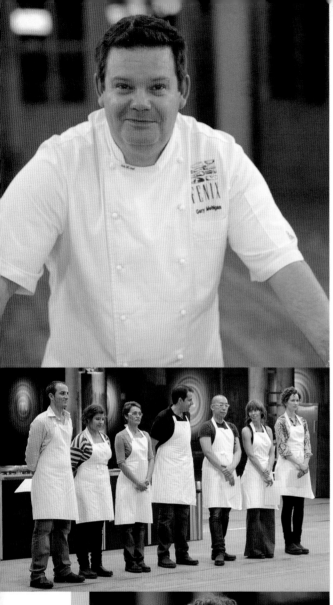

Gary Mehigan

With his two thriving restaurants, Fenix and Maribyrnong Boathouse, among the finest dining experiences in Melbourne, Gary's cooking credentials command attention. His natural leadership qualities also come to the fore in the MasterChef kitchen, where he mentors, encourages and teaches every hopeful contestant.

The winners of the signature dish challenge gained the opportunity to cook Gary's favourite recipe, beef Wellington. He described it as golden pastry, perfectly cooked beef and a simple red wine sauce to help it go down; Alvin, rather more poetically, described it as "a work of art". The two top contestants would be the first to go through to the Top 24. Claire and Jimmy triumphed, although Jimmy hadn't been at all confident about his "nappy-folded" pastry.

Claire blitzes the opposition and amazes George. "Who would've thought a lawyer could cook? I'll come to your lawyer party."

Serves **6–8**
Preparation 1¹/₂ **hours**
Cooking 1¹/₂ **hours**

BEEF WELLINGTON

800g centre-cut beef fillet*
10 slices prosciutto or jamón
1 tbs Dijon mustard
3 egg yolks
375g good-quality frozen puff
   pastry block, thawed
VEAL JUS
1 tbs olive oil
1kg small chopped beef bones
2 eschalots, thinly sliced
6 black peppercorns
1 clove garlic, bruised

4 sprigs thyme
1 bay leaf
80ml (¹/₃ cup) port
200ml red wine
1L (4 cups) veal stock
20g butter, chopped
CREPES
150g (1 cup) plain flour
2 eggs
375ml (1¹/₂ cups) milk
60g butter, melted
1 tbs finely chopped chives

1 tbs chopped flat-leaf parsley
1 tsp finely chopped tarragon
MUSHROOM LAYER
20g dried porcini mushrooms*
200g Swiss brown mushrooms
2 eschalots, finely chopped
1 clove garlic, finely chopped
40g butter, chopped
2 tbs chopped flat-leaf parsley
1 tbs finely chopped tarragon

1 **To make veal jus,** preheat oven to 200°C. Heat oil in a large ovenproof frying pan over medium heat.
   Add bones and cook, turning, for 8 minutes or until lightly browned. Place in oven and roast for
   25 minutes or until caramelised. Remove from oven and drain off all but 1 tbs fat.
   • Add eschalots, peppercorns, garlic, thyme and bay leaf to the pan and cook, stirring, over medium
   heat for 3 minutes or until eschalots are golden. Add port and wine and simmer for 5 minutes until
   liquid has reduced by two-thirds. Transfer to a large saucepan. Add stock and bring to boil. Skim any
   scum from surface. Simmer on medium heat for 40 minutes until liquid reduces to 500ml (2 cups).
   • Strain jus through a fine sieve into a small clean pan. Season with salt. Just before serving, reheat
   jus over medium heat and gradually whisk in butter to enrich jus and give it sheen.
2 **To make crêpes,** process flour, eggs, milk, 1 tbs of the butter and ¹/₂ tsp salt in a food processor until
   smooth. Transfer to a jug and rest for 15 minutes. Stir in chives, parsley and tarragon.
   • Heat a little butter in a 25cm non-stick frying pan over low–medium heat. Pour 80ml (¹/₃ cup)
   batter into pan and swirl to cover base. Cook for 1 minute or until lightly browned underneath. Turn
   over and cook for 1 minute or until golden. Transfer to a plate lined with baking paper. Repeat with
   remaining butter and batter. (You need 4 crêpes – the first is never perfect, so this quantity makes 6.)
3 **To make mushroom layer,** place porcini mushrooms in a bowl. Cover with boiling water and leave for
   15 minutes. Drain well and rinse. Process porcini and Swiss brown mushrooms, eschalots and garlic in
   food processor, occasionally scraping down side of bowl, until finely chopped (but not smooth).
   • Heat butter in a large frying pan over medium heat. Add mushroom mixture and stir for 5 minutes
   or until moisture has evaporated and mixture is thick. Stir in herbs. Season with salt and pepper.
4 **To seal and shape beef,** heat a greased heavy-based frying pan over high heat. Add beef and brown,
   turning, for 5 minutes. Season. For an even shape, wrap the hot beef fillet tightly in plastic wrap,
   twisting the ends to secure. Refrigerate until chilled, then remove plastic wrap.

1 **2** **3**

This classic mushroom mixture is called duxelles and has a rich, strong flavour. Along with the crêpes, it keeps the beef moist inside the pastry.

5 **To assemble beef Wellington,** place a 30 x 40cm sheet of baking paper on a work surface. Place 2 prosciutto slices on baking paper, end to end lengthwise, slightly overlapping, then repeat with a further 2 slices so they overlap the first. Repeat with the remaining 6 slices to form a rectangle. Spread mushroom mixture over prosciutto to form a compact layer about 21 x 25cm. Place fillet vertically on top and brush all over with mustard. Lift one end of baking paper and wrap prosciutto and mushroom firmly around beef.

• Place a second 30 x 40cm sheet of baking paper on a work surface. Place 4 crêpes, slightly overlapping, in 2 rows on baking paper. Trim outside edges to form 1 large square.

• Place the wrapped beef fillet in the centre of the crêpe square. Cut out small rectangles from each corner of the square to form a cross shape **(PIC 1)**. Lift narrow panels of trimmed crêpe and fold over fillet ends, then lift broad panels and wrap around fillet to encase. Wrap tightly in plastic wrap, twisting both ends to secure **(PIC 2)**. Freeze for 10 minutes to firm.

• Whisk egg yolks with a large pinch of salt. Roll out pastry to 30 x 38cm on a lightly floured sheet of baking paper. Place fillet in the centre of the pastry. Cut out small rectangles from each corner to form a cross shape **(PIC 3)** and reserve pastry trimmings. Lift narrow panels of pastry and fold over fillet ends, then lift broad panels of pastry and wrap around fillet to encase. The broad panels should overlap slightly; trim if necessary. Brush with egg yolk to seal.

• Place Wellington, seam-side down, on an oven tray lined with baking paper. Using a 5cm pastry cutter, cut out a round from reserved pastry, then, with a plain piping nozzle or sharp knife, cut a 1cm hole in the middle. Using a sharp knife, also cut out a 1cm hole from the centre top of the Wellington, cutting through the pastry only. Place pastry ring over the hole for the steam to escape. Brush Wellington all over with egg yolk mixture and freeze for 10 minutes.

6 **To cook beef Wellington,** preheat oven to 200°C. Bake for 25 minutes for medium–rare. To check, insert a meat thermometer into beef; the internal temperature should be 35°C (after resting, internal temperature will rise to 46–52°C). Or, pierce beef with a metal skewer, then touch skewer to inside of your wrist; it should feel just warm. Rest Wellington for 15 minutes before slicing and serving with jus.

YOU NEED an even-sized piece of beef, cut from the middle of the whole fillet. DRIED PORCINI MUSHROOMS are found in delis and specialist food shops.

Serves **8**
Preparation **30 minutes**
Cooking **25 minutes**

Philip's STRAWBERRY TART

Philip made this fantastic shortcrust tart with vanilla cream and strawberry coulis as part of the farm-fresh elimination challenge. He showed great attitude when the pressure of the MasterChef kitchen proved too much for his partner, Andrea, and he attempted to cook both their dishes. Gary had his fingers crossed but Philip's tart didn't need any help from luck. For Matt: "This tart screams summer and Wimbledon and strawberry shortcake. It stops being about the fruit and pastry and starts being about memories."

250g (1²/₃ cups) plain flour
80g (½ cup) icing sugar, plus
   extra, to dust

125g cold unsalted butter,
   chopped
1 egg, lightly beaten

500g strawberries, hulled, halved
375ml (1½ cups) pouring cream
1 tsp vanilla extract

1 Preheat oven to 190°C. Combine the flour and 55g (⅓ cup) of the icing sugar in a food processor. Add butter and process in short bursts until the mixture resembles fine breadcrumbs. Add the egg and process until mixture just comes together. Turn out onto the work surface, gather together and lightly press into a neat disc. Wrap in plastic wrap and refrigerate for 10 minutes.

2 Roll the pastry out between 2 sheets of baking paper until pastry is 3mm thick. Ease into a 22cm tart pan with a removable base. Place the tin on an oven tray and line with the baking paper. Fill with baking beans or uncooked rice and bake for 15 minutes. Remove paper and baking beans and return pastry to oven for a further 10 minutes or until golden. Cool completely.

3 Meanwhile, roughly chop 100g of the strawberries. Combine chopped strawberries, 1 tbs of the remaining icing sugar and 60ml (¼ cup) water in a saucepan. Bring just to the boil, reduce the heat to low and simmer, stirring occasionally, for 5 minutes or until the strawberries are pulpy and the mixture is thick and syrupy. Press through a fine sieve over a bowl. Refrigerate until cold.

4 When you are ready to serve, whisk the cream, remaining icing sugar and vanilla to stiff peaks, using an electric mixer. Gently fold through the strawberry coulis. Spoon into the pastry case, top with the remaining strawberries and dust with icing sugar.

DON'T OVERWORK the pastry in the processor or it will become tough and shrink during cooking.

Matt Moran

Matt Moran's food journey started 25 years ago, but today he is renowned as head chef and co-owner of Aria in Sydney and, since 2009, Brisbane. Raised on a New South Wales dairy farm, Matt's passion is for local, seasonal produce as the basis for a premium-quality menu. His cooking style is contemporary and innovative.

This challenge would gain six more contestants spots in the Top 24. They cooked along with Matt over four stages, being allowed just a little more time than the chef to complete each element to Matt's exacting Aria standards. The dish was pan-fried quail & potato gnocchi with sage butter and stages included dicing and blanching pumpkin, making potato gnocchi and boning quail. The plating had to be perfect and some hopefuls were heart-breakingly eliminated at the last moment. Peter, Jonathan, Aaron, Adam and Philip all made it through.

There is a buzz and intensity in the kitchen as the contestants race to keep up with Matt at every stage, but without letting standards drop.

Serves **6**
Preparation **40 minutes**
Cooking **1½ hours**

PAN-FRIED QUAIL & GNOCCHI

6 jumbo quails*
60ml (¼ cup) olive oil
180g unsalted butter, chopped
½ (about 600g) butternut
   pumpkin, peeled, seeded, cut
   into 1cm cubes
60ml (¼ cup) vegetable oil

¼ cup small sage leaves
40g (½ cup) shaved pecorino
   or parmesan
Chervil sprigs, to serve
GNOCCHI
300g (1 cup) rock salt*
800g desiree potatoes, scrubbed

75g (½ cup) plain flour, plus
   extra, to dust
2 egg yolks
1 tbs olive oil

1 **To make gnocchi,** preheat oven to 180°C. Spread salt to cover base of a small roasting pan and top
with potatoes. Roast for 1 hour, or until easily pierced with a skewer. Cool slightly and, when just cool
enough to handle, halve potatoes lengthwise and scoop flesh into a bowl.*
  • Pass potato flesh through a potato ricer* into a bowl **(PIC 1)**. Add flour and egg yolks **(PIC 2)** and
season. Stir with a spatula until mixture just comes together into a dough. (Don't overmix or gnocchi
won't be light.)
  • Line an oven tray with baking paper and dust with flour. Divide dough into 4. Using floured hands,
roll 1 portion into a 2cm-wide rope on a floured surface.
  • Using a floured knife, cut rope into 2cm pieces **(PIC 3)** and carefully place in a single layer on the
floured tray. Repeat with the remaining dough.
  • Fill a large bowl with iced water. Cook gnocchi in 2 batches in a large saucepan of boiling salted
water for 2 minutes or until gnocchi float to surface. Remove with a slotted spoon to iced water.
  • Drain gnocchi and toss with the oil. Place in a single layer on an oven tray lined with plastic wrap.
Cover and refrigerate until needed or for up to 1 day.
2 **To butterfly quails,** use a sharp knife or poultry shears to cut down either side of backbones and
remove. Place quails, skin-side down, on board and flatten breast bones with your palms. Cut around
rib cages, then remove, leaving the wings and legs intact. Season with salt and pepper.
  • Heat 1 tbs olive oil in a frying pan over medium heat. Add 2 quails, skin-side down, and cook for
2 minutes or until golden. Turn over, add 20g butter and cook until butter turns nut-brown.

- Basting quails with butter, cook for a further 2 minutes or until almost cooked through but still slightly pink in the centre. Transfer to an oven tray lined with paper towel and rest for 5 minutes. Meanwhile, cook remaining quails in 2 more batches using 1 tbs olive oil and 20g butter for each batch (wipe pan between batches). Loosely cover quails with foil.

3 **To cook pumpkin,** preheat oven to 150°C. Blanch pumpkin in boiling salted water for 2 minutes or until just tender. Drain and refresh under cold running water, then pat dry with paper towel.
   - Heat 1 tbs of the vegetable oil in a frying pan over high heat. Add pumpkin and cook, turning, for 3 minutes or until browned around the edges. Lift pumpkin out onto an oven tray and keep warm in oven. Keep the frying pan for the next step.

4 **To fry gnocchi and sage,** heat 1 tbs of the vegetable oil in the same frying pan over high heat. Add half the gnocchi, turning occasionally, for 3 minutes or until browned. Transfer to the oven to keep warm. Repeat with the remaining 1 tbs vegetable oil and gnocchi.
   - Melt remaining 120g butter in pan. When butter starts to foam, add sage and cook for 2 minutes or until crisp. Add gnocchi and toss to coat in sage butter.

5 **To serve,** arrange quails on plates and, with a slotted spoon, arrange gnocchi and pumpkin around quail. Spoon sage butter over the top and serve scattered with pecorino and chervil.

JUMBO QUAILS weigh about 200g and are available from selected supermarkets and butchers. If you prefer, ask your butcher to butterfly the quails. YOU CAN RE-USE the rock salt when making gnocchi again or use as pie weights for blind-baking pastry. COPY MATT'S KITCHEN STAFF and make a delicious snack out of the leftover potato skins. Cut them into wedges and fry in a little oil until crisp. POTATO RICERS are available from kitchenware shops. You could use a food mill (mouli) or a potato masher; however, a masher will not achieve the same fine texture.

Once you get the hang of the gnocchi they're very simple. Make extra to use in other dishes; uncooked, they freeze well for up to 2 months.

Matthew's LAYERED MOUSSE WITH STRAWBERRY SOUP

This Top 50 mystery box dish took Matthew into the Top 24. "It holds a special place in my memory. It was a blisteringly hot day, which made it difficult for a mousse to set during the short challenge. The freezers were being constantly opened and my heart was in my mouth as I lifted off the ring mould. Luckily, my mousse had set! Matt Preston described it as 'like eating chocolate and strawberry velvet', so I was very chuffed."

CHOCOLATE MOUSSE
150g dark chocolate (70% cocoa
  solids), chopped
1 x 5g leaf titanium-strength
  gelatine
1 egg

1 egg yolk
300ml pouring cream

CHOCOLATE GANACHE
200ml pouring cream
150g dark chocolate (70% cocoa
  solids), chopped

STRAWBERRY SOUP
110g (½ cup) caster sugar
8 strawberries, hulled, plus extra,
  to serve

1 To make chocolate mousse, fill a small saucepan one-third full with water and bring to a gentle simmer. Place the chocolate in a small heatproof bowl, place over the pan and stir until chocolate has melted (don't let the bowl touch the water). Set aside to cool slightly. Soften the gelatine in a small bowl of cold water for 3 minutes, then squeeze out excess water. Place the softened gelatine in a small bowl and set over a saucepan of simmering water until it becomes liquid.

2 Beat the egg and egg yolk in a large bowl for 5 minutes or until frothy. Stir in the melted chocolate then quickly mix in the gelatine. Whisk the cream to soft peaks and fold in. Place a 6cm-diameter, 6cm-high ring mould onto each of 6 serving dishes and fill with the mousse to 5mm below the top. Place in the fridge for 1 hour or until set.

3 To make chocolate ganache, bring the cream to a simmer in a small saucepan. Place the chocolate into a bowl, pour the hot cream over it and stir until the chocolate has melted. Leave ganache to cool until just warm, then pour over mousse in moulds. Return to the fridge for 30 minutes to set.

4 To make the strawberry soup, combine the sugar and 100ml water in a small saucepan and stir over low heat without boiling until the sugar dissolves. Bring to the boil, then remove from the heat and allow to cool slightly. Plunge the strawberries briefly into the syrup. Once coated, remove from the syrup and mix in a blender with 80ml (⅓ cup) of the syrup. Strain through a fine sieve, allowing it to drip through rather than pressing the mixture (it will take about 8 minutes) or it will become cloudy.

5 To serve, remove the rings to unmould each mousse. Pour a little strawberry soup around each mousse and serve with extra strawberries.

Serves **4**
Preparation **30 minutes**
Cooking **35 minutes**

Joanne's CREPE STACK WITH JAFFA MAZE & GRAND MARNIER SAUCE

The chocolate and fruit mystery box was also Joanne's ticket into the Top 24. "I cook with my heart, and my heart told me to do this. My husband is Dutch, so he loves anything orange! And my daughters are mad for chocolate. I kept thinking, 'I'm not going to come up with anything the judges like' and then, suddenly, the crêpes worked beautifully, the sauce was good and I even had time to plate it up. It's a crêpe stack in a chocolate orange maze... my girls love mazes, so I imagined them running through one to get to the crêpes."

Small mint sprigs, to serve

CREPES

225g (1½ cups) plain flour

3 eggs

410ml (1²/₃ cups) milk

40g unsalted butter

CREAM FILLING

375ml (1½ cups) pouring cream

1 tsp finely grated orange zest

1 tsp Grand Marnier

1 tsp caster sugar

JAFFA SAUCE

150g dark chocolate (70% cocoa solids), roughly chopped

80ml (1/3 cup) pouring cream

2 tbs orange juice

GRAND MARNIER SAUCE

150g (²/₃ cup) caster sugar

2 tbs orange juice

2 tsp finely grated orange zest

24 long thin shreds orange zest

60ml (¹/₄ cup) Grand Marnier

1 To make crêpes, combine flour, eggs, milk and a pinch of salt in a bowl and whisk until smooth. Strain through a sieve and leave to rest for 15 minutes.

2 To make cream filling, whisk together cream, zest, Grand Marnier and caster sugar until soft peaks form. Cover and refrigerate until required.

3 To make jaffa sauce, fill a small saucepan one-third full with water and bring to a gentle simmer. Place chocolate, cream and orange juice in a small heatproof bowl, place over pan and stir until chocolate has melted and mixture is smooth (don't let the base of the bowl touch the water).

4 To make Grand Marnier sauce, combine sugar and juice in a small saucepan. Stir over low heat until sugar dissolves. Stir in grated and shredded zest. Add Grand Marnier and increase heat to bring to the boil. Reduce heat to low–medium and simmer for 5 minutes until reduced and slightly thickened.

5 To cook crêpes, heat a very small non-stick frying pan or crêpe pan over medium heat. Grease the pan with ½ tsp butter. Pour 2 tbs batter into pan and immediately swirl the pan so the mixture spreads evenly. Cook for 1 minute or until golden underneath, then flip crêpe and cook for 1 further minute. Remove from pan, keep warm and use rest of batter to make 15 more crêpes.

6 Using an 8cm cutter, cut a neat round from each crêpe and discard trimmings. Place cutter on a serving plate to use as a mould. Place 1 crêpe into the mould and top with 2 tbs cream filling. Repeat to make a stack of 4 layers, finishing with a crêpe. Carefully lift off mould. Top each stack with a little cream filling and orange zest shreds. Top with a sprig of mint.

7 Drizzle jaffa sauce around the stack. Arrange mint sprigs around and serve with Grand Marnier sauce.

Kate's CHOCOLATE MOUSSE & MINTED SUGAR

Kate's mystery box mousse is perfect served with fresh strawberries. It's also extremely versatile: instead of mint you could use a shot of coffee or liqueur such as Kahlua. "Cooking this made me smile because it's always been a pleasure to cook it with my mum," says Kate.

250g dark chocolate (70% cocoa solids), chopped
4 eggs, separated

1 tsp vanilla extract
300ml pouring cream
4 mint leaves, plus extra

1½ tbs caster sugar
Whipped cream and mint leaves, to serve

1 Fill a small saucepan one-third full with water and bring to a gentle simmer. Place the chocolate into a small heatproof bowl, place over pan and stir until melted (don't let the bowl touch the water). Transfer to a large bowl.

2 Stir the egg yolks and vanilla into the chocolate. Whisk the cream to soft peaks and then gently fold through the chocolate mixture. Using an electric mixer, whisk the egg whites to soft peaks. Gently fold through the mixture until fully incorporated. Spoon into eight ½-cup (125ml) serving glasses and refrigerate for 4 hours or until well chilled and slightly firmed.

3 To make the minted sugar, pat the mint leaves with paper towel to absorb any excess moisture. Process the mint leaves and sugar in a small food processor until well combined. Serve the mousse with a dollop of whipped cream on top, sprinkled with the minted sugar and a mint leaf.

MAKE THE MINTED SUGAR with a mortar and pestle if you don't have a food processor. It is best prepared close to serving time: it will lose its vibrant colour if left to stand.

Neil Perry

The iconic Sydney chef and owner of the Rockpool Group had many of the contestants completely starstruck. His Rockpool restaurant has been named in the world's top 50 restaurants for seven years in a row, so it was fitting that his dish should be the final hurdle for the last contestants into the Top 24. The importance Neil places on quality is evident in all his dishes, whether they're created at his flagship restaurants, Rockpool, Spice Temple and Rockpool Bar & Grill Sydney and Melbourne, or in the MasterChef kitchen.

A momentous occasion calls for a momentous challenge and Neil's fish poached in coconut milk with garam masala and noodles was that challenge. Neil chose the dish because there were three separate elements to perfect: the flavour base of the coconut milk sauce; the noodles; and, of course, cutting perfect fillets from that snapper.

The final battle for a place in the Top 24: there isn't a person in the room whose nerves aren't frayed.

Serves **4**
Preparation **35 minutes**
Cooking **55 minutes**

FISH POACHED IN COCONUT MILK

2 x 1kg whole snappers,* cleaned
2 x 270ml cans coconut milk
8 kaffir lime leaves*
3cm piece ginger, cut into
   julienne (matchsticks)
2 tbs fish sauce
2 tbs grated palm sugar*
300g snow peas, trimmed
1 lime, juiced
60ml (¼ cup) coconut cream
1 cup Thai basil leaves*

TOMATO & CHILLI BASE
80ml (⅓ cup) vegetable oil
1 large onion, finely chopped
3 cloves garlic, crushed
2cm piece turmeric,* finely
   grated
5 green bird's-eye chillies
   (scuds),* finely chopped
5cm piece ginger, finely grated
6 vine-ripened tomatoes (900g),
   seeded, finely chopped

GARAM MASALA*
20g (¼ cup) cardamom pods
1 tsp cloves
1 tsp white peppercorns
2 cinnamon quills, crumbled
4 star anise, broken into pieces
SEMOLINA NOODLES
270g semolina flour*
2 tsp salt
2 eggs, plus 2 extra egg yolks
2 tsp vegetable oil

1 **To make tomato and chilli base,** heat oil in a heavy-based saucepan over low–medium heat. Add onion, garlic, turmeric, chillies and ginger, and stir for 3 minutes or until fragrant. Add 1 tsp salt, reduce heat to low and cook, stirring occasionally, for 30 minutes or until onion is dark golden and caramelised. Add tomatoes and cook for a further 10 minutes or until soft. Set aside.

2 **To fillet fish,** use a sharp filleting knife (these are thin-bladed and flexible) or a cook's knife to fillet each fish. Place 1 fish on a board. Make a cut just behind the fin, where the head finishes and the body starts, and run the knife from the top downwards to the bottom of the head **(PIC 1)**.

• Hold the knife flat on the backbone, then cut, running the knife along the length of the fish from head to tail. Retracing the cut, gradually work the knife along the top of the bones down to the vertebrae **(PIC 2)**. Slide the tip of the knife over the vertebrae, then over the rib cage until you reach the other side, then cut through skin to release fillet. While doing this, the knife must slide over the bones and never up into the flesh.

• Turn over the fish and repeat on the other side to remove the second fish fillet. Trim any bits of fin from each fillet. Repeat with the second fish.

• To remove pin-bones, place two fingers either side of each bone to firmly hold flesh. Holding tweezers in the other hand, grasp the bone firmly and pull it out.

• To remove skin from fillets, place a fillet skin-side down. Holding the tail end firmly, run the knife

horizontally between skin and flesh to separate **(PIC 3)**. Discard skin but keep the heads and bones for stock (keep in freezer in plastic bags for up to 2 months and add, frozen, directly to stock).

3 **To make garam masala,** place cardamom pods in a frying pan and stir over low–medium heat for 2 minutes or until fragrant and lightly toasted. Remove from pan. Repeat with remaining spices. Cool. Remove seeds from cardamom pods. Discard pods. Using a mortar and pestle or spice grinder, finely grind all spices. Garam masala will keep in an airtight container for up to 1 month.

4 **To make noodles,** combine flour and salt in a bowl and make a well in the centre. Add the eggs, yolks and oil. Using a fork, draw in flour until the mixture is thick, then work in remaining flour using your hands. Turn out onto the work surface and knead for 8 minutes or until dough is smooth; add extra flour if sticky. Wrap dough in plastic wrap and set aside for 30 minutes.

● Divide dough into 2 portions and keep one covered as you work with the other. Using a rolling pin, flatten one portion until 3mm thick and about 10cm wide – slightly narrower than your pasta machine. Set pasta machine at its widest setting (one) and feed the dough through. Fold the pasta in thirds, book style, turn at a right angle and feed through again. Repeat several times until pliable.

● Continue rolling, narrowing the settings on your machine one notch each time, until you reach setting five. Repeat with remaining dough. Use the fine noodle cutter to cut into strands. Hang over a clean broom stick resting between the backs of two chairs for about 30 minutes to dry.

5 **To make the sauce,** place tomato and chilli base and 1 tbs of the garam masala in a large wide saucepan or deep frying pan. Add coconut milk, kaffir lime leaves, ginger, fish sauce, palm sugar and 375ml (1½ cups) water and bring to the boil. Add fish fillets to the pan, cover and turn off the heat. Leave for 6 minutes; the heat of the liquid will cook the fish perfectly.

6 **To cook pasta and snow peas,** cook pasta in a saucepan of boiling salted water for 2 minutes until al dente. Drain. Cook snow peas in a saucepan of boiling salted water for 1 minute or until tender. Drain.

7 **To serve,** stir lime juice, coconut cream and half the basil into the fish curry. Twirl portions of pasta around a carving fork, then ease into bowls. Divide fish and curry among bowls and serve topped with snow peas and remaining basil.

IF YOU DON'T want to fillet fish, substitute 4 x 185g snapper fillets. KAFFIR LIME LEAVES, PALM SUGAR, THAI BASIL, TURMERIC AND SCUDS are all available from Asian grocers. If necessary, substitute ½ tsp ground turmeric for fresh and 1 long green chilli for 5 green bird's-eye chillies. BOUGHT GARAM MASALA, while not as fragrant as homemade, is available from supermarkets. SEMOLINA FLOUR (durum flour) is much more finely milled than the product labelled semolina or fine semolina. Try specialist food shops. You can use fine semolina, although it will produce a slightly drier noodle. Alternatively, use 300g bought spaghettini.

Chapter Two

DRUNKEN & BRUISED

Alvin's childhood memories take him to the first chef challenge, the teams battle to serve hungry punters in two Italian restaurants and, when Devon goes home after losing to The Eliminator, Australia "has never seen so many grown men cry". Phoebe has a birthday party, chocolate is in the mystery box and Jonathan gets inventive with goat.

Alvin's DRUNKEN CHICKEN & BRUISED SALAD

The recipe name might sound ominous, but Alvin's childhood memory is a very happy one. "This is my comfort food: my mum made drunken chicken if I was sick as a child, shredding chicken into a bowl with broth. As I grew older, it became a family meal with the whole chicken sitting in a large serving bowl of broth and the family tucking in, unabashed and unabated. The bruised salad shares the familiar storyline of a mother trying to get a little boy to eat his vegetables. I would get 10 cents every time I found and ate a 'red eye' (a snake bean that has been cut through the centre of the red seed)." This dish didn't get Alvin any coins from the judges but it certainly won their votes.

1 x 1.6kg chicken
1L (4 cups) Chinese rice wine
   (shaoxing)*
500ml (2 cups) mirin*
90g (¹/₃ cup) grated palm sugar*
Coriander leaves and steamed
   rice, to serve
SNAKE BEAN SALAD
90g (¹/₂ cup) grated palm sugar*
125ml (¹/₂ cup) lime juice

125ml (¹/₂ cup) fish sauce
75g (¹/₂ cup) roasted peanuts
6 cloves garlic, thickly sliced
80g dried shrimp*
12 cherry tomatoes, quartered
2 Lebanese cucumbers, peeled,
   thinly sliced into ribbons using
   a vegetable peeler
12 snake beans,* cut into 3cm
   lengths, blanched

4 red bird's-eye chillies, seeded,
   finely chopped
4 lime cheeks
CUCUMBER SALAD
1 Lebanese cucumber, peeled,
   seeded, cut into strips
¹/₄ cup chopped coriander leaves
2 tbs soy sauce
1 tbs sesame oil
2 tsp finely grated palm sugar

1 Place 3L water in a large saucepan and bring to the boil. Blanch chicken for 5 minutes, then drain.
2 Combine rice wine, mirin, sugar and 750ml (3 cups) water in large pan. Stir until sugar dissolves, then bring to the boil. Reduce heat to low, add chicken, cover and simmer for 45 minutes or until the juices run clear when the thickest part of the thigh is pierced with a skewer.
3 To make dressing for snake bean salad, whisk together palm sugar, lime juice and fish sauce.
4 Using a mortar and pestle, coarsely grind peanuts, garlic and shrimp. Transfer to a bowl and combine with tomatoes, cucumber, snake beans, dressing and half the chilli. Squeeze lime cheeks over the top.
5 Meanwhile, to make cucumber salad, combine all ingredients and leave for 15 minutes.
6 Remove the chicken from the pan and leave for 5 minutes or until cool enough to handle. Discard the skin. Warm the broth over medium–high heat.
7 Remove breasts and marylands from chicken and thickly slice meat. Divide among bowls, ladle broth over chicken and scatter with coriander and remaining chilli. Serve with salads and steamed rice.

SHAOXING, MIRIN, PALM SUGAR AND DRIED SHRIMP are available from Asian grocers. **SNAKE BEANS** can be found at good greengrocers.

Alvin's drunken and bruised was a stand-out dish of the entire series. "If I found this in a restaurant, I'd be going back twice a week." Gary

Jimmy's PRAWN PATIA WITH YELLOW DHAL & SAFFRON RICE

The childhood memory challenge was to bring much-loved food from the home and put it on the plate in the MasterChef kitchen. This traditional hot and sour dish is made in Bombay and Jimmy's mum still makes it for him every birthday; it's one of his earliest food memories.

1 tbs vegetable oil
1 large onion, puréed
5 cloves garlic
4cm piece ginger, grated
8 fresh curry leaves
6 red bird's-eye chillies
3 long green chillies
2 dried Kashmiri chillies
1 tsp tamarind concentrate
3 tsp white vinegar
1 tbs lemon juice

3 vine-ripened tomatoes, chopped
1 tsp ground coriander
1 tsp garam masala
½ tsp ground cumin
½ tsp ground turmeric
½ tsp amchur powder*
¼ tsp ground star anise
200ml fish stock
500g peeled green prawns
Coriander leaves and lime cheeks, to serve

SAFFRON RICE
400g (2 cups) basmati rice
1 pinch saffron threads
2 cinnamon quills
20g butter
YELLOW DHAL
150g (¾ cup) red lentils
25g ghee*
2 cloves garlic, crushed
2 tbs cumin seeds
1 tbs vegetable oil
1 small onion, chopped

1 To make saffron rice, put rice in bowl and cover with cold water. Soak for 1 hour. Drain well. Put in a saucepan with 500ml (2 cups) water, the saffron threads and cinnamon quills. Cover tightly and bring to the boil, then reduce heat to very low and cook for 15 minutes without removing lid. Remove from the heat and leave, covered, for 10 minutes. Add the butter and fork through.

2 To make yellow dhal, soak the lentils in cold water for 20 minutes, then drain. Melt ghee in a saucepan and cook garlic and cumin seeds over medium heat for 1 minute, stirring continuously until aromatic and starting to brown. Transfer to a small bowl. Heat oil in the same pan and cook onion over medium heat for 5 minutes or until soft and light golden. Add lentils and 375ml (1½ cups) water. Bring to a simmer, reduce heat to low, cover and cook for 50 minutes. Stir in the garlic-cumin mixture and cook, uncovered, for a further 20 minutes, stirring occasionally, until thick and creamy. Add more water if mixture starts to stick. Season with salt and sprinkle with coriander leaves to serve.

3 Meanwhile, heat the oil in a large heavy-based saucepan and cook onion over medium heat, stirring occasionally, for 8–10 minutes or until browned. Blend or process the garlic, ginger, curry leaves and chillies to a paste. Add to the pan and cook, stirring, for 5 minutes or until fragrant and slightly darker in colour. Add tamarind, vinegar and lemon juice. Cook over low heat for 5 minutes. Season with salt.

4 Add tomatoes to pan and bring to the boil. Reduce heat to low and cook for 5 minutes. Stir in the spices, then add fish stock and simmer, uncovered, for 10 minutes, stirring occasionally. Add the prawns and cook for 3 minutes or until they change colour and are cooked through. Serve with dhal, rice and lime cheeks.

AMCHUR POWDER is ground dried green mango and is available from Herbie's Spices in Sydney or by mail order (herbies.com.au). GHEE is clarified butter that is often used in Indian cooking. It cooks at a higher temperature than ordinary butter without burning and is widely available in tubs from supermarkets.

Adele's CROSTOLI WITH RICOTTA CREAM

These are Adele's "special-time" biscuits, made by her mum and dad to celebrate Christmas and birthdays. "This makes a big batch to go around – being Italian, that's what we do best! Mum could tell when we'd been at the biscuit tin by the crostoli crumbs round our mouths."

CROSTOLI
335g (2¼ cups) plain flour
55g (¼ cup) caster sugar
45g unsalted butter, melted and cooled
125ml (½ cup) white wine
1 tsp brandy

Vegetable oil, to deep-fry
Icing sugar and shredded orange zest, to serve
RICOTTA CREAM
250g fresh ricotta
75g (⅓ cup) caster sugar
1 orange, zested

300ml pouring cream
2 tbs chopped walnuts
2 tbs chopped dark chocolate (70% cocoa solids)
2 tbs chopped candied orange peel
1 tbs Cointreau or Grand Marnier

1 To make the crostoli, place the flour and sugar in a large bowl and make a well in the centre. Add the butter, wine and brandy. Mix with a wooden spoon and then with your hands to make a firm dough. Divide into 4 portions and keep covered.

2 Using a rolling pin, roll one portion out on a lightly floured surface to about 12cm wide and 3mm thick. Set your pasta machine at its widest setting (one), then feed the dough through. Fold the dough and feed it through again, repeating this about 10 times at this setting, until smooth and elastic. Keep rolling, narrowing the settings on your machine one notch at a time until you reach setting six. Repeat with remaining dough.

3 Using a fluted ravioli cutter, cut rolled dough into 3 x 11cm strips. Make a long cut down the centre of each strip and tuck one end through the cut to make a twist in the dough.

4 Fill a deep-fryer or large saucepan one-third full with vegetable oil and heat over medium heat to 180°C (or until a cube of bread turns golden in 10 seconds). Working in batches of 6 crostoli at a time, gently drop twists into the oil and fry for 15 seconds, turning halfway, until crisp and golden. Remove with a slotted spoon and drain on paper towel. Dust generously with icing sugar.

5 To make ricotta cream, using an electric mixer, beat the ricotta, sugar and orange zest until smooth. Beat in the cream, then stir in the remaining ingredients. Serve dollops of the cream, topped with shredded orange zest, with the crostoli.

STORE LEFTOVER crostoli in an airtight container for up to 3 days.

DRAIN the crostoli on paper towel after deep-frying, while you cook the next batch. It's an easy way to remove any excess oil.

Adele's face fell for a second when George teased her: "The only thing I'm missing here, and it's a pretty serious thing... is a little espresso."

Luke Nguyen

For four years, Luke Nguyen's Red Lantern has been named Sydney's Best Asian Restaurant. Born in a Thai refugee camp after his parents fled Vietnam as boat people, Luke has made a remarkable journey. Through his childhood he worked in his parents' noodle house and opened Red Lantern when he was just 23 years old.

For Alvin, with 90 minutes to replicate Luke's three-dish Vietnamese banquet, the challenge brings back special memories of a David and Goliath battle: "Yin and yang. Black versus white. The innocent monk pitted against the skilled Samurai... Luke was truly inspirational as a chef and a mentor. While the crowd went wild over his knife skills, I quivered trying to match up. It was a red-letter day for me and definitely something to tell the grandkids about."

The other contestants watched in awe. "Alvin's 15 minutes are up and it's like Jackie Chan starts. I've never seen two knives used like that," said Devon to camera.

Makes **10**
Preparation **40 minutes**
Cooking **15 minutes**

HANOI CRISP PARCELS

20g dried wood-ear mushrooms
20g bean vermicelli (glass
   noodles)
120g small green tiger prawns,
   peeled, deveined
100g pork mince
100g fresh crabmeat
¼ onion, finely diced
2 tsp sugar
1 tsp sea salt

1 tsp ground white pepper
2 tsp fish sauce
10 x 20cm round rice paper
   wrappers
1 egg white, lightly beaten
Vegetable oil, to deep-fry
1 bunch each of perilla,* mint and
   Vietnamese mint
1 iceberg lettuce, to serve

NUOC MAM CHAM*
125ml (½ cup) fish sauce
125ml (½ cup) rice vinegar
75g (⅓ cup) sugar
4 cloves garlic, chopped
2 bird's-eye chillies, thinly sliced
80ml (⅓ cup) lime juice

1 **To make nuoc mam cham,** combine the fish sauce, rice vinegar, sugar and 125ml (½ cup) of water in a saucepan. Stir over medium heat until almost at boiling point, then remove from heat and leave to cool. To serve, add the garlic and chilli, then stir in the lime juice.

2 **To make filling,** put mushrooms in a bowl, cover with cold water and soak for 20 minutes, then drain and thinly slice. Meanwhile, soak bean vermicelli in hot water for 5 minutes. Drain in a colander, rinse under cold water and drain well. Cut into 4cm lengths. Pound the prawns to a paste, using a mortar and pestle or a small food processor.

   • Put mushrooms, vermicelli, prawn meat, pork, crabmeat, onion, sugar, salt, white pepper and fish sauce in a large bowl. Mix with your hands for 3 minutes or until well combined.

3 **To fill,** working with one wrapper at a time, lower wrapper into a large bowl of warm water, drain off excess water and lay on a clean tea towel on a work surface. Place 1 heaped tbs of filling on the bottom edge of the rice paper. Fold the two sides inwards, overlapping them **(PIC 1)**. Roll up firmly from bottom and secure with a dab of egg white. Repeat until you have filled all the wrappers.

4 **To cook,** fill a deep-fryer or saucepan one-third full with vegetable oil and heat over medium heat to 180°C (or until a cube of bread turns golden in 10 seconds). Fry the parcels in 2 batches for 6 minutes or until browned and crisp. Remove with a slotted spoon and drain on paper towel. Serve with the fresh herbs and lettuce, and the nuoc mam cham for dipping.

PERILLA AND FISH MINT are herbs used widely in Asian cooking. You will find them at Asian grocers and greengrocers. THIS QUANTITY OF NUOC MAM CHAM is enough to serve with the parcels and the pancakes, opposite. Halve the quantity if you are only serving with the parcels.

HUE PANCAKES

100g peeled dried mung beans
  (moong dal)
80ml (1/3 cup) vegetable oil
200g green school (or small)
  prawns, peeled, deveined
2 cloves garlic, finely chopped
200g boneless pork belly, fat
  trimmed, thinly sliced

Green oak lettuce, to serve
1 bunch each of perilla,* mint,
  Vietnamese mint and fish
  mint,* and nuoc mam cham
  sauce, left, to serve
1 onion, thinly sliced into rings
500g mung bean sprouts

BATTER
90g (1/2 cup) rice flour
35g (1/4 cup) plain flour
1 tsp ground turmeric
160ml (2/3 cup) coconut cream
160ml (2/3 cup) soda water

1 **To make filling,** put the dried mung beans in a bowl, cover with cold water and soak for 20 minutes, then drain. Transfer to a steamer basket and steam over a saucepan of boiling water for 20 minutes.
  • Heat 1 tbs oil in a frying pan over medium heat. Add prawns and 1 tsp of the garlic and stir-fry for 2 minutes or until prawns change colour and are cooked through. Remove prawns and set aside.
  • Wipe the pan clean, heat 1 tbs oil and stir-fry pork and remaining garlic for 2 minutes or until cooked. Set aside.
2 **To make batter,** combine the flours, turmeric, 1/2 tsp salt, coconut cream and soda water. Whisk well and set aside for 10 minutes. Arrange lettuce leaves and herbs on a large platter.
3 **To cook pancakes,** heat 1 tsp of oil in a 20cm heavy-based non-stick frying pan over medium heat. When oil is hot, add about 60ml (1/4 cup) batter, enough to coat base of pan, swirling pan as you pour **(PIC 2)**. Add a few onion rings, sprinkle with a small handful of mung beans, followed by prawns, pork and bean sprouts. Fry for 2 minutes or until base is crisp and browned. Fold pancake in half to make it 'smile'. Repeat with remaining batter and filling to make 6 pancakes.
4 **To serve,** add perilla and mint leaves and roll in a lettuce leaf. Serve with nuoc mam cham for dipping.

A non-stick pan is vital for making perfect pancakes. You don't need to use much oil, or batter: just swirl the pan to coat the base.

PERILLA is found at Asian grocers and greengrocers. In Japanese cooking it is known as shiso.

2

Serves **2**
Preparation **30 minutes**
Cooking **35 minutes**

BARRAMUNDI CHARGRILLED IN LOTUS LEAF

4 dried lotus leaves*
2 barramundi (500g each),
  cleaned
2 spring onions, thinly sliced
  diagonally
1 lime, thinly sliced

PHU QUOC SEAFOOD SAUCE
60ml (¼ cup) vegetable oil
1 clove garlic, finely chopped
2cm piece ginger, finely chopped
½ stalk lemongrass, white part
  only, finely chopped
2 spring onions, thinly sliced

4 red eschalots, finely chopped
2 tsp fish sauce
1 tsp sugar
1 bird's-eye chilli, finely chopped
¼ tsp ground turmeric
2 tbs lime juice
2 tbs chopped dill

1 **To make phu quoc seafood sauce,** heat the oil in a saucepan over medium heat. Add the garlic,
  ginger, lemongrass, spring onions and eschalots and fry for 2–3 minutes or until fragrant. Reduce the
  heat to low and add the fish sauce, sugar, chilli and turmeric. Stir for 1 minute, then add the lime juice
  and dill. Remove from the heat and set aside to cool.

2 **To prepare fish,** soak the dried lotus leaves in hot water for 15 minutes, then drain. Meanwhile,
  marinate the fish with 2 tbs of the phu quoc sauce for 10 minutes. Soak the spring onions in a bowl of
  cold water until needed.

  • Arrange lime slices down each side of the fish, then place fish crosswise onto a lotus leaf, towards
  the bottom edge. Fold the bottom end up, covering the fish, then fold in the sides. Roll the fish in the
  lotus leaf, sealing both ends with toothpicks. (If the lotus leaf tears, wrap it in a second leaf.)

3 Heat a barbecue grill to high and chargrill the fish on each side for 15 minutes. Transfer to a platter.
  Using kitchen scissors, cut the lotus leaf down the middle **(PIC 1)** and open out the leaves like a
  parcel **(PIC 2)**. Garnish with drained spring onions and drizzle with the remaining phu quoc sauce.

DRIED LOTUS LEAVES can be
found at Asian grocers.

Callum's STUFFED ZUCCHINI FLOWERS

The first off-site team challenge threw everyone in at the deep end and ended in tears. The teams each ran an Italian restaurant in Sydney's Norton Street and the public couldn't wait to get inside. These zucchini flowers from Carpaccio were Matt Preston's dish of the day.

1 tbs olive oil
¼ leek, white part only, sliced
250g prawn meat
250g scallops
75g smoked scamorza,* grated
200g mozzarella, grated

18 zucchini flowers
Vegetable oil, to deep-fry
75g (½ cup) plain flour, to dust
Lemon wedges, to serve
BATTER
250g (1²/₃ cups) plain flour

80ml (⅓ cup) soda water
330ml (1⅓ cups) beer

1 Heat the olive oil in a frying pan and cook the leek over medium heat for 3–5 minutes or until soft but not coloured. Add the prawns and cook for 3 minutes, then add the scallops and cook a further 3 minutes or until they change colour and are cooked through. Cool slightly, then roughly chop the mixture in a food processor. Set aside to cool.

2 To make the batter, sift the flour into a large bowl, season with salt and pepper and make a well in the centre. Gradually add the soda water and then the beer, whisking until smooth. Add a little more soda water if necessary (batter should have the consistency of pouring cream). Cover with plastic wrap and leave to rest for 20 minutes.

3 Combine the cheeses with the prawn mixture and season to taste. Gently open a zucchini flower and fill with the prawn mixture. Twist the end to seal. Repeat with remaining flowers and filling.

4 Fill a deep-fryer or large saucepan one-third full with vegetable oil and heat over medium heat to 180°C (or until a cube of bread turns golden in 10 seconds). Working in 4 batches, dust the stuffed zucchini flowers with flour and shake off the excess. Dip into the batter, allowing excess to drain off, then gently drop into the oil. Fry for 2 minutes or until crisp and golden. Drain on paper towel. Serve with lemon wedges.

SCAMORZA is a semi-soft cheese similar to mozzarella. Smoked scamorza is available from delis.

Marion calmly worked the pizza ovens during the Norton Street challenge. When customers ordered a non-existent rocket and parmesan pizza (a menu mistake), Marion simply piled rocket salad on pizzas and created the dish herself.

Aaron's SPAGHETTINI WITH TUNA & BOTTARGA

Aaron remembers: "It was great fun cooking in the first team challenge. I got slammed on the pasta station and had a lot of trouble keeping up. One of my dishes was pasta with tuna and bottarga. While we were prepping for service I read the recipe and realised I had less time to prep than it was going to take to actually cook the tuna. This was a scary, scary challenge!" Hopefully, you can be a little more relaxed with time at home.

320g spaghettini
125ml (½ cup) extra virgin
   olive oil
1 clove garlic, chopped

1 tbs salted capers, rinsed
1 cup flat-leaf parsley leaves
250g yellow-fin tuna, cut into
   2cm dice

50g bottarga di muggine
   (smoked mullet roe), finely
   sliced
1 lime, zested

1 Bring a large saucepan of salted water to boil. Add the pasta and cook according to packet directions until al dente. Drain and keep warm.
2 Meanwhile, heat the oil in a large heavy-based frying pan over medium heat. Add the garlic, capers and parsley and cook for 1 minute or until fragrant. Add the tuna and cook over medium–high heat for 3 minutes or until the tuna is lightly seared.
3 Add the cooked pasta and toss together in the pan to coat well. Serve immediately, topped with bottarga and lime zest.

"If you make them wait long enough, they'll love anything!" Diners at two Italian restaurants waited patiently (and not so patiently) as kitchen chaos reigned.

Serves **4**
Preparation **45 minutes**
Cooking **30 minutes**

Marion's DUCK DUCK PIG

The duck duck pig produced Marion's first mystery box win of many. The theme was 'gourmet burger' and the contestants had to cook, and also name, their dishes. Marion says: "This is one lavish burger and certainly not diet material. I'd imagine it would be the sort of burger you'd order in a cosy little wine bar while sipping on a special glass of Pinot Noir."

2 tbs olive oil
1 onion, thinly sliced
2 tbs balsamic vinegar
2 tsp brown sugar
100g gruyère, sliced
4 hamburger buns, halved
1 tbs extra virgin olive oil
50g snow pea sprouts
1 bunch chives, trimmed

BURGERS
150g duck breast
200g pork shoulder, diced
50g pork fat, diced
1 tbs ground coriander
1 tbs fennel seeds
2 tsp salt
20g (¼ cup) Japanese panko
    breadcrumbs*

1 egg
TARRAGON MAYONNAISE
1 tbs Dijon mustard
3 egg yolks
150ml light olive oil
2 tbs chopped tarragon

1 To make burgers, remove skin from duck breast and keep on one side. Dice duck meat and mix with pork shoulder, pork fat, coriander, fennel and salt. Put through a mincer or finely chop in a food processor using the pulse button. Mix mince with breadcrumbs and egg and shape into 4 patties about 8cm in diameter.
2 To make mayonnaise, whisk together mustard and egg yolks until creamy. Whisking continuously, gradually add oil, drop by drop at first, then in a thin, steady stream until thick and emulsified. Stir in tarragon and season to taste. Cover and refrigerate until required.
3 Heat half the olive oil in a frying pan over low heat and add the onion. Cook for 20 minutes or until caramelised. Stir in the balsamic vinegar and sugar and season to taste.
4 Heat the remaining oil in a separate frying pan and fry the duck skin until crisp, then chop finely. Cook the burgers in the oil and duck fat over medium heat for 10 minutes, turning once, until cooked through. Lay a slice of gruyère over each cooked burger and cook briefly under a hot grill to melt.
5 Toast the buns and drizzle with extra virgin olive oil. Place sprouts and chives onto the bottom half and top with burger. Top with caramelised onions and sprinkle with crispy duck skin. Drizzle with the mayonnaise to serve.

PANKO BREADCRUMBS are coarse, dry Japanese breadcrumbs. They are available from the Asian food section of most large supermarkets or from specialist Asian food shops. For this recipe you could substitute fresh breadcrumbs.

"This really is the burger with the lot... the wonderful fragrant acidity of the béarnaise-style mayonnaise and beautiful crunchy duck crackling."

Matt Preston

Courtney's ONE-ARMED BANDIT SALMON BURGERS WITH HERBED MAYONNAISE

Courtney's mystery box burger perfectly blended her love of great flavours and practicality. "This is a cocktail-party burger that can be eaten with one hand, leaving the other free for a glass of wine or beer. I made a mayonnaise, too, full of capers, herbs and lemon zest."

½ baguette
1 tbs olive oil
1 clove garlic, halved
2 x 180g skinless, boneless
   salmon fillets, cut into 12 slices
1 ripe avocado, mashed
8 pitted kalamata olives, finely
   chopped

2 large dill pickles, sliced
½ cup shredded iceberg lettuce
HERBED MAYONNAISE
1 egg yolk
2 tsp lemon juice
1½ tsp white wine vinegar
½ tsp Dijon mustard
100ml olive oil

1 tsp finely grated lemon zest
1 tsp chopped capers
2 tsp chopped dill pickle
2 tsp chopped fresh herbs

1 To make the mayonnaise, whisk together egg yolk, lemon juice, vinegar and mustard until creamy. Mixing continuously, gradually add oil, drop by drop at first, then in a thin, steady stream until thick and emulsified. Stir in the remaining ingredients, season with salt and pepper and set aside.

2 Heat a large frying pan over medium–high heat. Cut the baguette into 24 slices, each about 1cm thick. Brush both sides of each slice with oil. Toast in the hot pan for 1 minute on each side or until golden. While still hot, rub the cut garlic clove over one side of each slice.

3 Heat the frying pan over medium–high heat. Season the salmon and cook for 2 minutes, then turn over and cook for 30 seconds.

4 Spread avocado over half the toast. Top with olives, pickles, lettuce and salmon. Drizzle with the herb mayonnaise and top with the remaining toast.

USE A MIXTURE of any fresh herbs to flavour the mayonnaise. Try tarragon, chives, parsley, dill or basil.

Serves **4**
Preparation **35 minutes**
Cooking **1 minute**

Callum's TUNA TATAKI WITH WASABI AVOCADO

Callum had been flying quietly under the radar before he came up with this dish in the Japanese invention test. Gary was amazed: "This is absolutely drop-dead gorgeous... Silky smooth avocado, tuna lightly seared so it has that slightly caramelised taste and then the great meaty saltiness of that sauce."

300g pkt pickled daikon*
160ml (2/3 cup) soy sauce
125ml (1/2 cup) rice wine vinegar
4 pieces sashimi-grade tuna, each cut to 3 x 4 x 10cm
1 tbs wasabi powder*
1 ripe avocado
1 cucumber
1 tbs salmon roe
100g enoki mushrooms
Micro herbs, to serve

1 Roughly chop half the daikon and combine with soy sauce and vinegar. Place in a shallow non-reactive dish, add the tuna and marinate for 10–15 minutes, turning occasionally.
2 Meanwhile, combine wasabi powder with 3 tsp water to make a paste. Mash the avocado with a fork and mix into the wasabi paste.
3 Use a vegetable peeler to cut 4 long thin strips from the cucumber. Stand one strip on its side on a piece of baking paper and bring the ends together to make a circle. Fill with mashed avocado and top with a dollop of salmon roe. Repeat to make 4 cucumber avocado rounds.
4 Preheat a chargrill pan over high heat. Drain the tuna, then sear, turning, for 45 seconds or until just coloured on all sides. Set aside to rest and cool for 2 minutes.
5 Place the mushrooms in a heatproof bowl and cover with boiling water. Leave for 1 minute, then drain and refresh in iced water. Drain and pat dry with paper towel. Cut the remaining daikon and cucumber into julienne (matchsticks).
6 To assemble, arrange the daikon, cucumber and mushrooms along the centre of each plate. Dress each with 3 tsp of the marinade. Slice the tuna and arrange over the vegetables, then place an avocado round on top in the centre. Scatter micro herbs sparingly around the plate.

DAIKON AND WASABI POWDER are available at Asian grocers.

Philippa Sibley

World-renowned pastry chef Philippa Sibley has recently launched a café and dessert bar at Il Fornaio in Melbourne's St Kilda. Philippa was appointed head pastry chef at Circa, the Prince, in 2005 and then took the reins at Bistro Guillaume in 2009. She is known in the industry as the "Queen of Desserts" and was the first woman to be named *The Age Good Food Guide* Chef of the Year, for her work at three-hatted Ondine.

Callum's reward for his Japanese invention test win was to cook off against Philippa, making her caramel parfait glacé with salted peanut caramel and milk chocolate cream. The dish, with its tempered chocolate plaques, brought gasps of awe from the mezzanine and obviously tasted as good as it looked.

After judging Philippa's dish Gary said, "I feel slightly embarrassed about revealing this score: 10 out of 10".

"This dessert is no piece of cake." The youngest contestant transforms spectacularly from dish-washing student to celebrity chef challenger.

Serves **8**

Preparation **2 hours + overnight freezing**

Cooking **20 minutes**

CARAMEL PARFAIT GLACE

CARAMEL MOUSSE
600ml thickened cream

150g (²/₃ cup) caster sugar

1 vanilla bean, split, seeds
scraped

135g liquid glucose

50g cold unsalted butter,
chopped

6 x 2g leaves gold-strength
gelatine

55g (¹/₄ cup) caster sugar, extra

10 egg yolks

CHOCOLATE CHANTILLY CREAM
250g good-quality milk
chocolate, chopped

300ml thickened cream

SALTED PEANUT CARAMEL
180ml (³/₄ cup) thickened cream

80g liquid glucose

150g caster sugar

50g cold unsalted butter,
chopped

100g (²/₃ cup) salted peanuts,
coarsely chopped

¹/₄ tsp sea salt

PEANUT DACQUOISE
150g (1 cup) salted peanuts

240g (1¹/₂ cups) icing sugar,
sifted

80g (²/₃ cup) ground almonds

5 egg whites

100g caster sugar

CHOCOLATE PLAQUES
200g good-quality milk
chocolate

1 **To make caramel mousse,** grease a 3cm deep, 28 x 18cm pan and line with baking paper. Using an electric mixer, whisk 300ml of the cream to soft peaks. Cover and refrigerate until needed.

2 Heat a heavy-based saucepan over medium heat and sprinkle in 1 tsp of the caster sugar. When dissolved, gradually add the remaining sugar, stirring continuously until dissolved and lightly golden.
  • Combine remaining cream, vanilla seeds and 115g glucose in another saucepan and bring to the boil over medium–high heat. Slowly pour into the caramel, whisking until combined. Whisk in the butter.
  • Meanwhile, soak the gelatine leaves in a small bowl of cold water for 5 minutes, then drain and squeeze out the excess liquid. Whisk into the mixture until dissolved.
  • Strain through a fine sieve into a bowl. Place over another bowl filled with ice and water and leave to cool, whisking occasionally.

3 Combine the extra caster sugar, 1¹/₂ tbs water and the remaining glucose in a small saucepan. Stir over medium heat to dissolve the sugar, then bring to the boil. Cook for 5 minutes or until it reaches 118°C on a sugar thermometer. Remove from the heat and let the bubbles subside.
  • Meanwhile, using an electric mixer, beat the yolks on moderate speed until frothy. With the mixer running, pour the syrup down the side of the bowl. Increase the speed to high and whisk until pale, doubled in size and cooled.
  • To finish the mousse, fold together the 2 cooled mixtures, then fold in the whipped cream. Pour into the lined pan and freeze for 8 hours or overnight or until very firm.

4 **To make chocolate chantilly cream,** melt the chocolate and keep warm to the touch. Using an electric mixer, whisk the cream to soft peaks. Quickly whisk half the warm chocolate into the cream to lighten the mixture. Immediately whisk in the remaining chocolate. Cover and refrigerate.

5 **To make salted peanut caramel,** combine cream and glucose in a saucepan and bring to the boil. Set aside and keep warm. Heat a heavy-based saucepan over medium heat and sprinkle in 1 tsp of the caster sugar. When dissolved, gradually add remaining sugar, stirring continuously, until dissolved and light golden. Slowly pour the hot cream mixture onto the caramel, whisking until combined.
   • Whisk in the butter, then set over another bowl filled with ice and water and leave to cool until slightly thickened. Fold in the peanuts and salt. Refrigerate until needed.

6 **To make peanut dacquoise,** preheat oven to 160°C. Grease a large oven tray and line with baking paper. Finely grind peanuts in a food processor, then mix with icing sugar and ground almonds.
   • Using an electric mixer, whisk the egg whites to soft peaks. Gradually add the caster sugar, whisking continuously until stiff and glossy.
   • Gently fold nut mixture into meringue, taking care not to lose volume. Spread over oven tray to about 1cm thick (larger than the area of the mousse). Bake for 8 minutes or until crisp on top but slightly soft in centre. Place a piece of baking paper over dacquoise and carefully invert onto a flat oven tray. Peel off the paper and cool for 5 minutes.
   • Remove mousse from freezer and invert onto slightly warm dacquoise. Press down lightly to just stick together. Lift tin off mousse, leaving paper in place **(PIC 1)**. Return to the freezer until needed.

7 **To make chocolate plaques,** melt chocolate in a small heatproof bowl over a pan of barely simmering water (don't let the bowl touch the water). Pour two-thirds of the melted chocolate onto a cool, clean work surface (marble is ideal) and spread around until it begins to thicken and feels cool to the touch. Return cooler chocolate to the warmer chocolate in the bowl. Stir until completely combined. It should read about 26°C on a sugar thermometer (it will feel cool on the side of your little finger).

8 Stick eight 4 x 30cm strips of acetate plastic to the work surface with sticky tape (to prevent moving). Spread chocolate onto the strips with a palette knife **(PIC 2)**. When just set to the touch but still slightly pliable, mark strips into 10cm lengths and then cut through chocolate and acetate with scissors. You need 16 neat strips, plus extra for breakages. Refrigerate until needed.

9 Remove tray from freezer and peel off paper. Trim away excess dacquoise and, using a long hot knife, cut mousse into 8 neat 4 x 10cm bars with clean straight edges.

10 **To serve,** smear a little peanut caramel onto a cool plate to stop dessert sliding around. Place mousse bar onto the caramel, dacquoise-side down. Peel plastic off a chocolate plaque and place on top, shiny-side up. Use 2 teaspoons dipped in hot water to make quenelles of chantilly cream, and place 3 onto the plaque. Place a teaspoon of peanut caramel between the quenelles. Place another plaque on top **(PIC 3)**, shiny-side up (without putting fingerprints on chocolate). Serve immediately.

Serves **12**
Preparation **20 minutes**
Cooking **15 minutes**

Courtney's SALT & PEPPER SEAFOOD WITH LIME MAYONNAISE

Courtney took a risk with seafood for the children's party challenge. Half the votes would be from children, half from adults, so she made a dish to appeal to both. This was perfect as easy, delicious party food. "Once you've peeled the prawns, this is quick to prepare and cook for the masses. I made a mayonnaise to go with it and added lime for a boost."

1.2kg snapper fillets, pin-boned
Vegetable oil, to deep-fry
200g (1 cup) rice flour
35g (¼ cup) cornflour
35g (¼ cup) plain flour
1 tbs sea salt flakes, plus extra
3 tsp ground white pepper

3 tsp ground black pepper
2 tsp Chinese five-spice, plus
   extra, to serve
24 medium green king prawns,
   peeled, deveined, tails intact
Chopped red chilli, coriander and
   lime wedges, to serve

LIME MAYONNAISE

2 egg yolks
1 tbs Dijon mustard
1 lime, zested and juiced
125ml (½ cup) light olive oil
125ml (½ cup) vegetable oil

1 To make lime mayonnaise, process yolks, mustard and lime zest and juice in a food processor until well combined. With the motor running, gradually add oils, drop by drop at first, then in a thin steady stream until thick and emulsified. Season with salt and pepper. Thin with 2 tbs water.
2 Remove skin from fish and cut fish into strips a similar size to the prawns.
3 Fill a wok one-third full with oil and heat to 180°C (or until a bread cube turns golden in 10 seconds).
4 Combine flours, salt and spices in a large bowl. Dust a quarter of seafood in flour mixture, shake off excess, then gently drop into oil and fry for 1½ minutes, turning halfway, or until light golden and just cooked through. Remove with a slotted spoon. Drain on paper towel. Sprinkle with a little extra sea salt and five-spice. Dust, fry and season the remaining seafood in 3 more batches.
5 Serve with chilli, coriander, lime wedges and mayonnaise.

One hundred and fifty children and parents voted for their favourite party food from the red and blue teams.

Serves **4**
Preparation **20 minutes**
+ **3 hours refrigeration**
Cooking **40 minutes**

Jimmy's BUTTER CHICKEN

Jimmy was thrown into a dilemma by Phoebe's request for curry at her birthday party. Although she liked spicy food, he knew many of the other children might not. "This is a special child-friendly butter chicken with the spices used in a subtle way to enhance the sweet and salty flavours that children's tastebuds enjoy."

140g (½ cup) Greek-style
  yoghurt
3cm piece ginger, finely grated
2 cloves garlic, crushed
1 lemon, juiced
2 tbs olive oil
¼ cup chopped coriander, plus
  extra leaves, to serve

2 tbs garam masala
800g chicken thigh fillets, cut
  into 3cm-wide strips
2 tbs ghee*
2 onions, thinly sliced
1 tsp ground turmeric
2 long red chillies, seeded, finely
  chopped

1½ tbs tomato paste
260g (1 cup) passata (sieved
  puréed tomatoes)
300ml pouring cream
1 bunch mint, finely chopped
Basmati rice and pappadams,
  to serve

1 Combine yoghurt, ginger, garlic, lemon juice, oil, half the coriander and half the garam masala in a large bowl. Season with salt and pepper, add chicken and toss to coat. Cover with plastic wrap and refrigerate for 3 hours.

2 Preheat a lightly oiled barbecue or chargrill pan over medium–high heat. Remove chicken from marinade and cook in 2 batches for 6 minutes, turning once, or until almost cooked through.

3 Heat ghee in a large saucepan over medium heat. Add onions, turmeric, chillies, tomato paste and remaining garam masala and cook, stirring, for 5 minutes or until onions are soft. Add passata and cook for 5 minutes or until slightly thickened. Reduce heat to low, add cream, mint and remaining coriander and cook, stirring, for 2 minutes. Add chicken and simmer, stirring occasionally, for 15 minutes or until sauce thickens. Scatter with extra coriander and serve with rice and pappadams.

GHEE is clarified butter that is often used in Indian cooking. It cooks at a higher temperature than ordinary butter without burning. Ghee is widely available in tubs from supermarkets.

Makes **12**
Preparation **20 minutes**
Cooking **25 minutes**

Dom's CUPCAKES

Dom's cupcakes were a triumph of creativity over adversity. As captain of the red team for the children's party challenge, Dom used up so much time helping out the rest of the team that he was still making his cupcakes minutes before the guests arrived. His inspired idea was to put out the icing and decorations and hold a "decorate your own cupcake" party.

225g (1½ cups) self-raising flour
220g (1 cup) caster sugar
125g unsalted butter, softened,
   chopped
2 tsp vanilla extract

1 orange, zested
2 eggs
2 tbs milk
Silver balls and Smarties
   (optional), to decorate

CREAM CHEESE ICING
125g unsalted butter, softened
250g cream cheese, softened
1 orange, zested
320g (2 cups) icing sugar, sifted

1 Preheat oven to 180°C. Line a 12-hole (80ml / ⅓-cup) muffin pan with 12 paper cases.
2 Using an electric mixer, beat flour, sugar, butter, vanilla, orange zest, eggs and milk on low speed until combined. Increase speed to medium–high and beat for a further 5 minutes or until light and fluffy.
3 Divide batter among paper cases and bake for 20 minutes or until golden and a skewer inserted into the centre comes out clean. Leave for 5 minutes, then transfer to a wire rack to cool completely.
4 To make cream cheese icing, using an electric mixer, beat butter, cheese and orange zest until pale and doubled in volume, then, while beating, gradually add sugar and beat until just incorporated. (If icing is a little soft, refrigerate for 15 minutes to firm.)
5 Spread icing over cupcakes. Decorate with silver balls and Smarties, if using.

Matt and Phoebe ponder over which way the votes will be cast.

Skye's CRISPY DUCK & RASPBERRY SAUCE

"Rock and roll, Skye, rock and roll!" was George's comment on this winning mystery box dish. "Perfectly cooked duck and a stand-out gorgeous sauce that brings it all together. And what I love most are these crispy, flavoursome fennel tops. A very clever dish."

140g red cabbage, thinly shaved
1 tbs duck fat
1 tbs olive oil
4 free-range duck breast fillets
    (about 300g each)
Vegetable oil, to fry

Fronds from 1 fennel bulb
2 tbs extra virgin olive oil
2 tsp red wine vinegar
RASPBERRY SAUCE
200ml red wine
50ml red wine vinegar

1 bacon rasher, halved
1½ tbs caster sugar
100g butter, cubed
½ tsp freshly ground black
    pepper
1 punnet (125g) raspberries

1 Put the cabbage in a large bowl, cover with cold water and set aside. Divide the duck fat and olive oil between 2 large frying pans and warm over low heat. Season the duck breasts and place two in each pan, skin-side down. Cook for 10 minutes to render the fat. Increase the heat to medium–high and cook for 4 minutes or until the skin is crisp. Turn breasts over, reduce heat to medium and cook for a further 5 minutes or until golden and duck is cooked medium–rare. Transfer to a warm plate to rest. Keep the duck juices from the pan.

2 To make raspberry sauce, put wine and vinegar in a small saucepan. Bring to the boil and cook for 5 minutes over medium–high heat or until reduced to 100ml (pour into a heatproof measuring jug to check: if not correct, return to pan and reduce further). Set aside in the saucepan.

3 Heat a small frying pan over low–medium heat and cook the bacon for 10 minutes to render the fat. Remove bacon from pan and tip out all but 1 tbs of fat. Add 1 tbs of duck pan juices and pour in the red wine reduction. Add the sugar and stir over low–medium heat until dissolved.

4 Add the butter to the pan a cube at a time, whisking continuously, until all butter is incorporated and the sauce is glossy and has thickened slightly. Season with salt and the black pepper and leave to cool slightly. Pour over the raspberries and leave to macerate in a warm place.

5 Pour 3cm vegetable oil into a small saucepan and heat over medium heat to 180°C (or until a cube of bread turns golden in 10 seconds). Add the fennel fronds and cook for 10 seconds or until crisp. Remove with a slotted spoon and drain on paper towel.

6 Drain the cabbage and pat dry with paper towel. Combine the extra virgin olive oil with the red wine vinegar and season with salt and pepper. Toss the cabbage with the dressing.

7 To serve, spoon the raspberry sauce onto the plate and smear slightly. Place duck breast on top, skin-side up. Make a little pile of raspberries on one side and a pile of cabbage on the other. Top cabbage with crisp fennel fronds. Serve immediately with remaining sauce on the side.

IF YOU HAVE A MANDOLIN, use it here to shred the cabbage. Otherwise, use a large sharp knife. **DUCK FAT** can be bought from good butchers and some large supermarkets.

Makes **6**
Preparation **25 minutes**
Cooking **20 minutes**

Carrie's CHOCOLATE & RASPBERRY SOUFFLES WITH LAVENDER CREAM

Carrie was thrilled when she opened the mystery box to find chocolate and raspberries. "I have always been passionate about desserts. This is a classic dish I love making for my friends and it really represents my style of cooking. When my name was called for tasting as one of the top dishes, it was definitely my proudest moment in the competition."

20g unsalted butter, melted and cooled
55g (¼ cup) caster sugar
60g unsalted butter, chopped
200g dark chocolate, chopped

1 punnet (125g) raspberries
3 egg yolks
6 egg whites
80g caster sugar

LAVENDER CREAM
300ml pouring cream
1 tbs caster sugar
1 tsp dried lavender,* chopped

1 To make lavender cream, use an electric mixer to whisk the cream, sugar and lavender to soft peaks. Cover with plastic wrap and refrigerate for the flavours to develop.

2 Preheat oven to 180°C. Grease six 1-cup (250ml) ovenproof ramekins with melted butter and sprinkle with caster sugar to coat the base and sides. Shake out the excess sugar. Fill a small saucepan one-third full with water and bring to a gentle simmer. Place the butter and chocolate in a small heatproof bowl, place over the pan and stir until melted (don't let the bowl touch the water). Transfer chocolate mixture to a large bowl and set aside.

3 Put raspberries in a blender and blend to a smooth purée. Pass through a fine sieve, pressing with the back of a spoon to remove the seeds. Stir raspberry purée and egg yolks into the chocolate mixture.

4 Using an electric mixer, whisk egg whites to stiff peaks, then gradually add sugar and whisk until you have a thick, glossy meringue.* Gently stir one-third of the meringue into the chocolate mixture to loosen, then use a large metal spoon to fold in the remaining meringue. Fold until meringue is fully incorporated with no white streaks, taking care not to lose volume.

5 Divide the mixture evenly among the ramekins without spilling onto the rim of the dish (or soufflés will stick to rim and not rise evenly). Place on an oven tray and bake for 18 minutes or until well risen. Serve immediately with the lavender cream.

DRIED LAVENDER FLOWERS are available from The Essential Ingredient or Herbie's Spices in Sydney (mail order: herbies.com.au).

RUB THE MERINGUE between your fingertips to make sure all the sugar crystals have dissolved.

"This is a lovely light soufflé, but what's really clever about this dish is the subtlety of the lavender cream. It does something extraordinary to the flavour of that chocolate." Gary

Makes **6**
Preparation **30 minutes**
+ 25 minutes refrigeration
Cooking **25 minutes**

Fiona's CHOCOLATE GANACHE TARTS WITH RASPBERRIES & LAVENDER CREAM

This was Gary's favourite dish of the series. "What I loved about Fiona's chocolate tart was its simplicity. It ticked all the right boxes: texture, flavour and, of course, irresistible to look at. For me, the combination of soft, luscious bitter chocolate ganache and the subtle lavender-scented chantilly cream was a dream set in crumbly pastry. An utter knock-out."

300g (2 cups) plain flour
150g cold unsalted butter, chopped
1 punnet (125g) raspberries

GANACHE
400g dark chocolate (70% cocoa solids), chopped
250ml (1 cup) pouring cream
50g unsalted butter, chopped

LAVENDER CREAM
300ml thickened cream, whipped
1 tsp dried lavender,† chopped

1 Preheat oven to 180°C. Lightly grease six 10cm tart pans with removable bases. Process flour and butter in a food processor until mixture resembles breadcrumbs. Add 80ml (⅓ cup) cold water and process until mixture just comes together. Form dough into a ball, then divide into 6 portions and shape each into a disc. Roll out each disc on a sheet of lightly floured baking paper until 3mm thick. Line the pans with pastry, trim edges and chill for 20 minutes.

2 Place the pans onto 1 large or 2 smaller oven trays and line each with baking paper. Fill with dried beans or uncooked rice and bake for 15 minutes, then remove beans and paper and bake for a further 10 minutes or until pastry is golden and dry. Set aside to cool.

3 To make ganache, place chocolate in a heatproof bowl. Place cream and butter in a small saucepan and bring almost to the boil. Pour mixture over chocolate and stir until melted and smooth. Spoon ganache among tart shells, then refrigerate for 5 minutes or until ganache just sets.

4 To make lavender cream, using an electric mixer, whisk cream to soft peaks. Fold lavender petals into cream, then top each tart with a spoonful and some raspberries.

DRIED LAVENDER FLOWERS are available from The Essential Ingredient or Herbie's Spices in Sydney (mail order: herbies.com.au).

Fiona demonstrated how to make her chocolate ganache tarts during the last Masterclass of the series. She made full use of her helpful sous-chefs, Gary and George.

Jonathan's GOAT CURRY & FROZEN YOGHURTS

Skye surprised all by choosing goat for the curry invention test. Jonathan won the challenge with spiced frozen yoghurts and pappadam praline, combining both salty and sweet.

4 bird's-eye chillies, chopped
2 long red chillies, chopped
4cm piece ginger, chopped
4 garlic cloves, chopped
1 lime, zested
80ml (1/3 cup) ghee
1kg goat or lamb leg or shoulder,
    cut into 2cm cubes
2 tsp black mustard seeds
1 tbs garam masala
10 fresh curry leaves
1 tbs coriander seeds

3 cardamom pods
2 cloves
2 tsp ground black pepper
1 Indian bay leaf
1 cinnamon quill
1 pinch saffron threads
200g freshly grated coconut
100g plain yoghurt
1 1/2 tsp sugar, or to taste
FROZEN YOGHURTS
1kg plain yoghurt
1 lime, juiced

2 tbs caster sugar, or to taste
1 tsp ground cinnamon
1/2 tsp saffron threads
1 tsp garam masala
PAPPADAM PRALINE
Vegetable oil, to shallow-fry
2 pappadams
110g (1/2 cup) caster sugar
1 tbs cumin seeds
1/4 cinnamon quill
Fresh curry leaves, lime wedges
    and pappadams, to serve

1 To make frozen yoghurts, place yoghurt, lime juice and sugar in a bowl. Whisk to loosen and dissolve the sugar (taste and add a little more sugar if you like). Transfer to an ice-cream maker and churn for 35 minutes or until smooth and frozen.

2 Meanwhile, put cinnamon, saffron and garam masala in three separate small bowls. Add 1 tbs hot water to each and put in fridge to chill. When yoghurt is frozen, divide into thirds and add one spice mixture to each portion. Place into separate bowls, cover and freeze until needed.

3 To make pappadam praline, heat 1cm oil in a frying pan over medium heat until hot. Fry the pappadams one at a time for 3 seconds each side or until puffed and crisp. Drain on paper towels. Break up the pappadams and place on a foil-lined oven tray. Heat a large saucepan over high heat, sprinkle 75g (1/3 cup) of the sugar into saucepan and allow to melt and caramelise. Sprinkle rest of sugar into pan, and swirl pan to mix together. Cook, without stirring, until dark caramel. Remove pan from heat, add cumin and cinnamon and swirl pan to combine. Pour caramel over pappadams and leave for 10 minutes to cool and harden. Break roughly and pulse in food processor to coarse crumbs.

4 Combine the chillies, ginger, garlic and lime zest in a small food processor and process until almost smooth; set aside. Heat half the ghee in a large pan and brown the goat in 2 batches over high heat for 1–2 minutes. Transfer to a bowl with a slotted spoon.

5 Heat remaining ghee in same pan and fry paste over medium heat for 2 minutes or until fragrant. Add black mustard seeds, garam masala, curry leaves, coriander seeds, cardamom pods and cloves and cook for 2 minutes. Return goat to the pan, add 500ml (2 cups) water and simmer, covered, over low heat for 30 minutes, stirring occasionally. Add black pepper, bay leaf, cinnamon, saffron and coconut. Cook for 1 hour or until goat is tender. Uncover and cook for 5–10 minutes or until thickened slightly. Remove from heat and stir in yoghurt. Season with salt, pepper and sugar.

6 Garnish curry with fresh curry leaves and lime wedges. Serve with frozen yoghurts sprinkled with praline, with extra pappadams on the side.

Serves **4**
Preparation **35 minutes**
Cooking **25 minutes**

Courtney's SPICED GOAT WITH EGGPLANT, NAAN & MINT RAITA

Matt Preston renamed this the "goat souvlaki". With only 10 extra ingredients to grab from the pantry Courtney had to think quickly in the curry invention test. "I had made naan bread before – so I decided to make it as a canapé topped with spiced goat, crispy eggplant and mint yoghurt. I came close to winning but just missed out to Jonathan's great dish."

2 x 300g goat or lamb
  backstraps, trimmed
350g eggplant, cut into 5mm-
  thick slices
Vegetable oil, to shallow-fry
4cm piece ginger, cut into
  julienne (matchsticks)
2 tbs olive oil
Mint leaves, to serve

MARINADE
1 tsp fennel seeds
1 tsp cumin seeds
1 tsp black mustard seeds
1 tsp coriander seeds
1 tsp ground turmeric
2 tbs plain yoghurt

BLACK SESAME NAAN
70g (¼ cup) plain yoghurt

1 egg, lightly beaten
125ml (½ cup) milk
300g (2 cups) plain flour
Olive oil, to grease
1 tbs black sesame seeds

MINT RAITA
140g (½ cup) plain yoghurt
¼ cup shredded mint leaves

1 To make the marinade, toast whole spices in a frying pan over medium heat for 1 minute or until fragrant. Using a mortar and pestle, finely grind spices. Reserve 1 tsp spice mixture for raita. Combine the remainder with turmeric, ½ tsp salt and the yoghurt in a non-metallic bowl. Add goat and toss to coat. Refrigerate for 20 minutes. Bring the meat to room temperature 10 minutes before cooking.

2 To make naan, place 2 large oven trays in oven and preheat to 250°C. Combine yoghurt, egg and milk in a bowl. Sift flour with 1 tsp salt into a separate bowl. Make a well in the centre, add yoghurt mixture and stir until mixture comes together, adding a little flour or water if necessary. Knead on a lightly floured surface for 1 minute or until smooth. Divide dough into 8 balls. Using greased hands, lightly coat dough in oil. Cover with plastic wrap. Rest for 10 minutes.

3 Meanwhile, to make raita, combine yoghurt, mint and reserved spice mixture in a small bowl. Season with salt and pepper and refrigerate until needed.

4 Using your palms, flatten naan dough until 5mm thick. Sprinkle with sesame seeds and press lightly into the dough. Place 4 naans on each tray and bake for 4 minutes or until puffed and golden. Wrap in a clean tea towel to keep warm.

5 Sprinkle eggplant with 1 tbs salt. Place in a colander and leave for 10 minutes for salt to draw out moisture. Brush off excess salt and pat dry with paper towel.

6 Fill a large frying pan 1cm deep with vegetable oil and heat over medium–high heat. Fry eggplant in 3 batches, refilling pan with oil each time, for 2 minutes each side or until soft and golden. Remove with a slotted spoon. Drain on paper towel. Refill pan with vegetable oil and reduce heat to medium. Fry ginger for 1 minute or until crisp. Drain on paper towel.

7 To cook goat, scrape off excess marinade. Heat olive oil in a frying pan over medium–high heat. Cook goat for 2 minutes each side for medium-rare. Rest for 5 minutes. Cut into 1cm-thick slices. Divide eggplant and goat among plates. Scatter with mint and ginger and serve with naan and mint raita.

Justin North

Australian chefs "don't come much bigger than this". Justin North is chef and owner of Sydney's Bécasse and Etch restaurants; he is also passionate about ethical eating and sustainable produce. Justin opened his first restaurant, Bécasse, in Sydney's Surry Hills in 2001. He garnered instant accolades and two chef's hats. In 2009 he was named *Sydney Morning Herald Good Food Guide* Chef of the Year. His advice to any new chef is to use the best produce and techniques to create the most excitement in all the senses.

For his cook-off against Jonathan, Justin's dish was caramelised confit and roast rack of suckling pig. "This is a very good summary of the basic skills any chef should have: butchery, making a confit, two different types of cooking and creating very precise flavours."

"I think he's dreaming," said Jonathan.

Jonathan, in chef whites for the first time, is "anxious as all hell, but also excited". Justin "seems to be moving really fast, but without actually moving!"

Serves **4**
Preparation **1 hour 15 minutes + overnight refrigeration**
Cooking **2 hours 15 minutes**

CARAMELISED CONFIT & ROAST RACK OF SUCKLING PIG

4 cloves garlic
8 sprigs thyme
2 sprigs rosemary
1 bay leaf
12 coriander seeds
8 black peppercorns
2 star anise
1 cinnamon quill
60g (1/2 cup) sea salt flakes
200g piece of pork belly from
   suckling pig*
1.5L (6 cups) duck fat*
1 tbs olive oil
2 racks of 6 cutlets from
   suckling pig*
4 black figs, cut into pieces
Baby cress, to garnish

ROAST MARRON TAIL
2 live marrons,* sedated 2 hours
   beforehand
60ml (1/4 cup) grape seed oil
4 cloves garlic
4 sprigs thyme
2 tbs sea salt

FENNEL AND GINGER PUREE
60ml (1/4 cup) grape seed oil
50g unsalted butter
1 onion, finely sliced
4cm piece ginger, grated
2 fennel bulbs, chopped
1/2 cup (125ml) white wine
3 tsp Pernod
125ml (1/2 cup) chicken stock
60ml (1/4 cup) thickened cream

SPICED JUS
2 tbs grape seed oil
40g unsalted butter
2 eschalots, sliced thinly
2 cloves garlic, sliced thinly
4cm piece ginger, sliced thinly
1 tsp honey
2 sprigs thyme
1 bay leaf
1 tsp Chinese five-spice
125ml (1/2 cup) white wine
310ml (1 1/4 cups) veal jus

1 Preheat oven to 100°C. Using a mortar and pestle, pound garlic, herbs and spices until crushed and aromatic. Rub in the salt. Massage the aromatic salt into the pork belly.
  • Heat duck fat in a large ovenproof saucepan to 90°C. Submerge pork belly in duck fat and cover with a round of baking paper **(PIC 1)**. Bake in oven for 1 hour or until soft. Remove from the oven. Transfer pork belly to a tray and cover with another tray. Weigh down with cans or a brick and refrigerate overnight.

2 Preheat the oven to 190°C. Cut pork belly into 4 rectangular pieces. Heat oil in an ovenproof frying pan over medium–high heat and cook pork belly, skin-side down, for 5 minutes or until crisp and golden. Place in oven for 5 minutes to warm through.

3 **To make fennel and ginger purée,** heat the oil and butter in a heavy-based saucepan over medium heat until foamy but not coloured. Add onion, ginger and fennel and cook for 10–15 minutes or until soft and translucent but not coloured.
  • Add wine and cook for 8 minutes or until reduced and syrupy. Add Pernod and stock and simmer for 5 minutes or until vegetables have broken down and softened. Add cream and bring to the boil. Season with salt, cool slightly and purée in a blender until very smooth. Pass through a fine sieve.

4 **To make spiced jus,** heat oil and butter in a heavy-based saucepan over medium heat until foamy but not coloured. Add eschalots, garlic and ginger and cook for 6–8 minutes or until lightly golden. Add honey, thyme, bay leaf and five-spice and cook for 1 minute. Add wine and cook for 5 minutes or until reduced and syrupy, then add the veal jus. Bring to a simmer, reduce the heat slightly and cook gently for 3 minutes or until a sauce-like consistency.

5 **To cook racks and marron,** preheat oven to 190°C. Season racks with salt and pepper. Heat remaining oil in a heavy-based ovenproof frying pan over medium heat. Gently caramelise the skin of the racks for 5 minutes to start the crackling process **(PIC 2)**. Place in the oven and cook for 6 minutes.
  • Cut marron tails from bodies. Tie a spoon to the tails to keep straight while roasting **(PIC 3)**. Heat oil in a heavy-based frying pan over high heat. Add marron tails and caramelise for 1 minute on each side. Remove from heat and add garlic, thyme and salt. Cover with foil and roast in oven for 5 minutes. Set aside the pork and marron to rest for 3 minutes. Cut the shell from the marron and slice the flesh into medallions. Carve the racks into cutlets.

6 **To serve,** spoon a few pools of warmed fennel and ginger purée onto plates. Arrange the pork belly, cutlets and marron tail on the plate. Add the figs, drizzle with the jus and finish with some baby cress. Serve remaining fennel and ginger purée and sauce separately.

A GOOD BUTCHER will provide you with these particular cuts from a suckling pig and the duck fat. **THE DUCK FAT** can be strained through a sieve and stored in the fridge to use again. **MARRONS** will need to be ordered from a good fishmonger. Put in the freezer for 2 hours before cooking to sedate humanely.

Chapter Three

MUD CRABS & MANGOES

Mud crabs and finger limes in the mystery box inspire Peter to magic. Flags of the world are flown and Aaron does his Mexican dance. Curtis Stone helps the red and blue teams ambush families in the supermarket, pizzas are perfected and then Marion gets inventive with mangoes and fish sauce and faces Frank Camorra in a Melbourne laneway.

Peter's CHILLI CRAB WITH CRISP CHIPS

When the lid came off this mystery box, Matt Preston decided it was "the yummiest we've seen yet". Mud crabs and finger limes, mushrooms and radicchio: all looked spectacular. Peter had never cooked mud crab before and he fired up the wok. "With 5 minutes to go, I just cut up some pasta and threw it in a pan to crisp up, so there was something nice to dip in the sauce." At tasting, the judges adored this dish, but Peter was modest as ever: "I'm just happy to be up the front. I don't have to win, because I've got all the accolades I need today." He won anyway, and even got a kiss from Jimmy.

1 live mud crab (about 1.4kg),
    sedated 2 hours beforehand*
2 tbs peanut oil, plus extra to
    shallow-fry

5 long red chillies, finely sliced
400g can diced tomatoes
3 finger limes, flesh removed
2 tbs brown sugar

270ml can coconut cream
2 sheets fresh pasta*

1 Use a large knife or cleaver to cut crab in half. Pull off the top part of the shell and reserve. Remove the gills. Break off the legs and claws and crack with a cleaver or the back of a knife. Reserve shell.
2 Heat a wok over high heat and heat the oil. When hot, add 4 of the chillies and fry for 3 minutes or until soft. Add the tomatoes and stir well, then add the crab shells. Cook for 5 minutes for the flavour to infuse.
3 Add half the lime flesh with the sugar and coconut cream and cook for 5 minutes. Remove the shells from the sauce and add the claws. Cook for 2 minutes and add the legs. Cook, stirring occasionally, for a further 6 minutes or until the crab has changed colour. Season with plenty of salt and pepper.
4 Meanwhile, cut the pasta sheets into small triangles. Heat about 3cm peanut oil in a large frying pan over medium–high heat and fry the pasta for 1 minute or until crisp and golden.
5 Add the remaining lime and fresh chilli to the crab and serve with the crisp chips.

PUT THE CRAB in your freezer for 2 hours before cooking to sedate it humanely. **USE WONTON WRAPPERS** instead of pasta to make the chips, if you like.

CHOP THE CRAB in half with one clean cut with a large sharp knife or cleaver. Then pull off the top shell and remove the gills.

Serves **4**
Preparation **45 minutes**
+ 2 hours freezing
Cooking **20 minutes**

Jimmy's MUD CRAB PARATHA WITH CHILLI OIL & EGG YOLK

This was the speediest mystery box challenge ever – 25 minutes to think, create and cook. Jimmy decided to be realistic about the time constraints and create a quick and easy snack, using the crabmeat as a filling for his trademark bread.

1 live mud crab (about 1kg),
   sedated 2 hours beforehand*
225g (1½ cups) plain flour
1 pinch salt

2 tbs coconut cream
2 tbs peanut oil, plus extra to
   shallow-fry
5 red chillies, sliced

20g butter
4 eggs

1 Bring a large saucepan of salted water to the boil. Add the whole crab and cook for 10 minutes or until just slightly undercooked. Plunge into iced water to stop the cooking process, then drain well. Cut the crab into portions and extract all the meat from the legs and body. Set aside half the meat for another recipe.*

2 Mix the flour and salt in a large bowl and make a well in the centre. Add the coconut cream and 125ml (½ cup) water to make a soft dough. Knead on a lightly floured surface until smooth.

3 Divide the dough into 4 equal portions and roll each piece into a round about 3mm thick. Scatter crabmeat over half of each round, then fold over to enclose the crabmeat. Roll out again to about 4mm thick.

4 To make the chilli oil, heat the oil in a small saucepan and cook chillies over medium heat for 2 minutes or until beginning to blister. Remove from the heat and set aside.

5 Heat 1cm oil in a large frying pan over medium–high heat. Cook the dough for 2 minutes each side or until puffed and golden. Drain on paper towel. Melt the butter in a separate frying pan, break the eggs into the pan and cook over medium–high heat for 2 minutes or until the whites have set.

6 Serve the paratha topped with the eggs and drizzled with chilli oil.

PUT THE CRAB in your freezer for 2 hours before cooking to sedate it humanely. **YOU WILL ONLY** need half the crabmeat, so put in an airtight container and freeze it immediately, or double the other ingredients to serve 8. Alternatively, use 150g already prepared fresh crabmeat from a fishmonger.

Joanne's MUSHROOM & RADICCHIO LASAGNE

When Joanne opened the mud crab mystery box her mind went blank. "I completely forgot how to prepare crab! Soon there was crab absolutely everywhere, so I wiped the bench, tried to calm down and started again." This layered lasagne was quick and simple, but the flavours are lovely. The burnt butter drizzled over the top took it to the judges' tasting table.

80g butter	3 fresh lasagne sheets
1 tbs olive oil	1 cup shredded radicchio, plus
500g button or mixed*	extra, to serve
mushrooms, sliced	75g gorgonzola

1 Melt 20g of butter with the oil in a frying pan and cook the mushrooms until soft. Season to taste and set aside.

2 Using an 8cm round cutter, cut 4 rounds from each sheet of pasta. Cook in batches in a large pan of boiling salted water for 1 minute or until al dente. Lift from the water with a slotted spoon and drain on a clean tea towel.

3 Melt another 20g of the butter in a frying pan over low heat. Add the radicchio and cook, stirring, until wilted. Season to taste.

4 Arrange the wilted radicchio on 4 plates. Lay a pasta round on the radicchio. Top with one-third of the mushrooms and gorgonzola. Layer another pasta round on top and then more mushrooms and gorgonzola. Place the final pasta round on top and add the remaining mushrooms and gorgonzola.

5 Melt the remaining butter in a frying pan over medium heat and cook for 3 minutes until browned. Drizzle over the lasagne. Finish with shredded radicchio and freshly ground black pepper.

YOU CAN BUY great packs of mixed mushrooms in some good supermarkets and greengrocers. They are perfect for a recipe like this.

Serves **4**
Preparation **40 minutes**
+ 3 hours freezing
Cooking **35 minutes**

Aaron, Matthew & Joanne's CHICKEN TACOS, TOMATO SALSA & JALAPENO GRANITA

Aaron loved the flag invention test. "My eyes instantly locked on the Mexican flag. I was holding my breath that no other team would choose it, so it was a great relief when I got to do the Mexican dance. This dish was similar to one of my audition dishes, and Jo and Matthew were happy to have fun and take some risks. The granita was originally supposed to be a jelly... Had the jelly worked out, who knows? We might not have won."

5 vine-ripened tomatoes,
   quartered, seeded

1 tbs Tabasco sauce

2 tsp ground cumin

1 lemon, juiced

2 tbs tomato paste

2 jalapeños,* halved, seeded

4 chicken breast fillets

8 tortillas

Coriander leaves and lemon
   wedges, to serve

JALAPENO GRANITA

2 tbs olive oil

8 jalapeños, halved, seeded

2 green capsicums, seeded

1 lime, juiced

GUACAMOLE

2 avocados, seeded

1 lemon, zested, juiced

2 tbs finely chopped coriander

1/2 tsp ground cumin

1/2 tsp Tabasco sauce

TOMATO SALSA

3 vine-ripened tomatoes, seeded,
   finely chopped

1 red onion, finely chopped

2 tbs finely chopped coriander

2 tbs olive oil

1 tsp Tabasco sauce

1 tsp ground cumin

1 Process tomatoes, Tabasco, cumin, lemon juice, tomato paste, jalapeños and 250ml (1 cup) water in a food processor until smooth. Combine half the tomato mixture with chicken. Cover and refrigerate for 30 minutes. Strain remaining tomato mixture through a fine sieve into a saucepan. Bring to the boil. Simmer for 10 minutes or until thickened slightly into a tomato sauce. Cool and set aside.

2 Meanwhile, to make jalapeño granita, preheat oven to 220°C. Combine oil, jalapeños and capsicums in a bowl and season. Place on an oven tray and roast for 20 minutes until tender. Purée capsicum mixture and 250ml (1 cup) water in a food processor. Strain through a fine sieve into a tray with lime juice. Freeze for 3 hours, scraping with a fork every 30 minutes to break up ice crystals.

3 To make guacamole, process all ingredients in a food processor until smooth, then season.

4 To make tomato salsa, combine all ingredients in a bowl and season.

5 Preheat an oiled chargrill pan over medium heat. Remove chicken from marinade and cook for 4 minutes or until browned underneath. Turn and cook for a further 5 minutes or until cooked through. Rest for 5 minutes, then slice. Wipe pan clean and toast tortillas for 30 seconds each side. Top with chicken, salsa and guacamole. Scatter with coriander, drizzle with the tomato sauce and serve with lime wedges and granita.

JALAPENOS are a type of hot chilli and are available from good greengrocers.

Serves **4**
Preparation **1 hour**
Cooking **1 hour**

Marion, Adam & Peter's SMOKED CHICKEN & WONTONS WITH BLACK BROTH

Matt Preston thinks that the flag invention test saw some of the best dishes of the competition. "Here's a favourite of mine. Delicate but punch-packing broth came loaded with perfectly smoked chicken and little wontons. The dish was a triumph of Peter's technique, Marion's bold flavours and Adam's restraint. It nearly won them the challenge."

110g (1/2 cup firmly packed) dark brown sugar
100g (1/2 cup) white rice
8 star anise, broken
1 orange, zested
400g chicken breast fillets
1 bunch Chinese broccoli (gai lan), trimmed, shredded
150g oyster mushrooms

BLACK BROTH
3 cloves garlic, peeled

2 tbs black peppercorns
2 tbs olive oil
1.5L (6 cups) chicken stock
3 star anise
125ml (1/2 cup) dark soy sauce
125ml (1/2 cup) Chinese rice wine (shaoxing)*
60ml (1/4 cup) rice vinegar
2 tbs dark brown sugar

GARLIC CHIVE PASTE
1 bunch garlic chives,* chopped

1 clove garlic, roughly chopped
1 tsp brown sugar
60ml (1/4 cup) peanut oil

WONTONS
200g chicken thigh fillets, roughly chopped
1 bunch garlic chives, chopped
1 tsp Chinese rice wine (shaoxing)
1 clove garlic, peeled
16 gow gee pastry wrappers*

1 To make black broth, using a mortar and pestle, pound garlic and peppercorns to a coarse paste. Heat oil in a large saucepan over high heat. Add garlic-peppercorn paste and cook, stirring, for 1 minute until fragrant. Add the remaining ingredients, bring to the boil, then simmer for 50 minutes, regularly skimming scum. Strain through a fine sieve into a clean saucepan. Cover and set aside.

2 Meanwhile, to smoke chicken, combine sugar, rice, star anise and orange zest in a bowl. Transfer to a wok lined with 2 layers of foil and heat over high heat for 5 minutes or until mixture starts to smoke. Reduce heat to medium, place a wire rack on top, then place chicken in a single layer on the rack. Cover with a lid and cook for 12 minutes, then turn and cook for a further 12 minutes or until chicken is cooked through.

3 To make the garlic chive paste, mix garlic chives, garlic, sugar and 1 tbs water in a food processor. With the motor running, add oil in a thin, steady stream until thick and emulsified, then season.

4 To make wontons, process chicken, garlic chives, rice wine and garlic in a food processor until minced. Season. Place 1 tsp chicken mixture in the centre of a gow gee wrapper. Brush the edge of the wrapper with a little water, then fold in half. Fold edge into pleats, then pinch together to seal. Repeat with the remaining wrappers and chicken mixture.

5 Bring black broth to the boil over medium heat. Add wontons, broccoli and mushrooms and cook for 5 minutes or until wontons are cooked through. Thickly slice chicken breasts. Divide wontons, vegetables and soup among bowls, top with chicken and serve with garlic chive paste.

CHINESE RICE WINE (SHAOXING) AND GARLIC CHIVES are available from Asian grocers. GOW GEE PASTRY WRAPPERS are available from selected supermarkets.

Jonathan, Claire & Philip's MOROCCAN CHICKEN WITH CHICKPEAS

Peter, who had won the mystery box and was choosing the teams for the flag invention test, seemed a little shocked when Jonathan not only recognised the Moroccan flag but then explained that it was his family heritage. Working with Claire and Phil, Jonathan created a beautiful bistro-style dish based on the classic Moroccan ras el hanout chicken.

140ml olive oil
2 tbs ras el hanout*
1 tsp harissa*
3 cloves garlic, 2 crushed, 1 thinly sliced
4 chicken marylands
1 onion, thinly sliced

1 tbs honey
1 large orange sweet potato (kumara), peeled, cut into 3cm pieces
500ml (2 cups) chicken consommé*
400g can chickpeas, rinsed

4 vine-ripened tomatoes, seeded, roughly chopped
1 cup coriander leaves, chopped
Thinly sliced preserved lemon rind,* to serve

1 Preheat oven to 180°C. Combine 60ml (¼ cup) oil, ras el hanout, harissa and crushed garlic in a bowl and season with salt and pepper. Add chicken and toss to coat. Heat 2 tbs oil in a frying pan over medium–high heat. Add chicken, skin-side down, and cook, turning, for 5 minutes or until browned.

2 Heat the remaining 2 tbs oil in a casserole over medium–high heat. Add sliced garlic, onion and honey and cook, stirring, for 5 minutes or until onions are soft. Add sweet potato, consommé and chicken and bring to the boil. Cover and roast for 25 minutes or until chicken is cooked through.

3 Using a slotted spoon, transfer chicken to a tray. Using a ladle, skim excess fat from the top of the broth. Stir in chickpeas, tomatoes and coriander. Divide among bowls, top with chicken and scatter with preserved lemon rind to serve.

RAS EL HANOUT ('top of the shop') is a Moroccan mix of up to 20 spices, from Herbie's Spices in Sydney or by mail order (herbies.com.au). **HARISSA** is a Tunisian chilli paste, available from supermarkets. **CHICKEN CONSOMME** is a clear broth made from richly flavoured stock, available from supermarkets.

PRESERVED LEMON is available from delis. The rind is the part that is used. Rinse a few wedges to wash off the brine, then cut off and discard the flesh and thinly slice the rind.

"Jonathan called on family memories back in Morocco for this succulent golden spice-rubbed chicken. Strips of preserved lemon add tang."

Matt Preston

Serves **4**
Preparation **50 minutes**
Cooking **5–10 minutes**

Alvin's PORK SCHNITZEL WITH COLESLAW

The pork schnitzel pressure test created panic in the minds of Alvin, Fiona and Daniel. Self-doubt abounded, and pork, beef and veal blurred into one awful meaty dilemma. The judges didn't ask for much: just simple homemade breadcrumbs and coleslaw with a perfect creamy mayonnaise. Not so easy when you're facing elimination.

4 x 80g pork leg steaks
300g sourdough bread, crusts
  removed, roughly chopped
1 tbs chopped flat-leaf parsley
1½ tbs chopped sage
1½ tbs chopped thyme
20g (¼ cup) finely grated
  parmesan
75g (½ cup) plain flour

2 eggs
2 tbs olive oil
40g butter
Lemon wedges, to serve
MAYONNAISE
1 egg
1 tbs Dijon mustard
2 tsp chardonnay (or white wine)
  vinegar

250ml (1 cup) olive oil
COLESLAW
1 carrot, peeled, cut into julienne
  (matchsticks)
¼ white cabbage (200g), finely
  shredded
½ red onion, finely sliced

1 To make mayonnaise, process the egg, mustard and vinegar together in a small food processor until creamy. With motor running, gradually add oil, drop by drop at first, then in a thin steady stream until thick and emulsified. Season to taste.

2 To make coleslaw, mix the carrot, cabbage and onion in a bowl. Add enough mayonnaise* to bind together and mix well. Set aside.

3 Using a meat mallet, pound the steaks to 5mm thick. Season with salt and pepper.

4 Place the bread in a food processor and pulse to form coarse crumbs. Combine the crumbs, herbs and parmesan in a bowl. Season the flour and spread onto a plate. Whisk the eggs in a shallow bowl.

5 Working with 1 piece at a time, dip a pork steak into the flour and shake off the excess. Dip into egg, then coat with breadcrumb mixture, pressing the crumbs on firmly with your fingertips. Refrigerate for 20 minutes to firm up.

6 Heat oil and butter in a large frying pan over medium heat. Cook the pork in 2 batches for 2 minutes each side or until browned and cooked. Drain on paper towel. Serve with coleslaw and lemon.

KEEP REMAINING MAYONNAISE in an airtight container in the fridge for up to 3 days.

Serves **4**
Preparation **50 minutes**
Cooking **35 minutes**

Jimmy & Aaron's HAWKER PRAWNS WITH ROTI & MINT CHUTNEY

For Curtis Stone's supermarket challenge the blue team ambushed a family who had lived in Singapore. Jimmy remembers: "They liked spicy food and we decided to remind them of the Singaporean hawkers. The best part of the day was watching their son enjoy this dish... He told us he wouldn't eat prawns, then quickly realised he liked the flavour of these."

2 bird's-eye chillies, chopped
1 tsp garam masala
1 tsp lemon juice
1 tsp Greek-style yoghurt
1 tsp chopped coriander stems
16 medium green prawns, peeled, deveined, tails intact

100g snow peas, trimmed, blanched
50g bean sprouts
1 tsp chopped coriander leaves

ROTI
450g (3 cups) plain flour
1 tsp salt

1 tsp Greek-style yoghurt
Vegetable oil, to shallow-fry

MINT CHUTNEY
1 cup mint leaves
2 tbs coriander leaves
95g (1/3 cup) Greek-style yoghurt

1 To make mint chutney, process the mint, coriander and yoghurt in a food processor until smooth. Season with salt to taste. Cover and refrigerate until ready to serve.

2 Combine the chillies, garam masala, lemon juice, yoghurt and coriander stems in a shallow non-metallic dish. Add the prawns and toss to coat. Marinate in the fridge for 20 minutes.

3 To make roti, sift the flour into a large bowl and add the salt. Make a well in the centre, add the yoghurt and 300ml water. Mix with a wooden spoon and then your hands to make a soft dough. Turn out onto a floured surface and knead for 1 minute. Roll the dough into 8 balls and roll out on a lightly floured surface to 2–3mm thick ovals or rounds. Heat 2cm oil in a large frying pan. Cook the roti over medium–high heat for 2 minutes each side or until puffed and golden brown. Drain on paper towels. Cover with foil to keep warm.

4 Preheat a barbecue flatplate to high heat and cook the prawns for 2 minutes or until they have changed colour and are cooked through.

5 To serve, arrange the prawns on a bed of snow peas, bean sprouts and chopped coriander. Drizzle the mint chutney around the edge of the plate and serve with roti.

The teams "ambushed" unsuspecting shoppers in the supermarket and went home with them to cook the family dinner. The contestants nicknamed this challenge "the home invasion".

Serves **4**
Preparation **20 minutes**
Cooking **35 minutes**

Alvin, Adam & Claire's POACHED CHICKEN WITH ASIAN COLESLAW

This dish from the supermarket ambush challenge was another that impressed Matt Preston. "Alvin's tender poached chicken was the hero, but the coleslaw also added loads of vibrancy, freshness and crunch, making this dish a great light lunch option."

110g (1/2 cup) caster sugar
1 lime, juiced, zest cut into strips
2 cinnamon quills
2 kaffir lime leaves, bruised
1 stalk lemongrass, white part
   only, bruised
400ml coconut cream
250ml (1 cup) chicken
   consommé*
800g chicken breast fillets

VINEGAR AND LIME DRESSING
110g (1/2 cup) caster sugar
60ml (1/4 cup) rice wine vinegar
1 lime, juiced
1/2 tsp sesame oil
2 tsp fish sauce
ASIAN COLESLAW
1 carrot, peeled, cut into julienne
   (matchsticks)
1 red onion, thinly sliced

2 spring onions, thinly sliced on
   the diagonal
120g (1 1/2 cups) finely shredded
   Chinese cabbage (wombok)
125g cherry tomatoes, quartered
2 tbs coriander leaves, plus extra,
   to serve

1 Heat sugar and 2 tbs water in a large saucepan over high heat and cook for 6 minutes, or until a golden caramel starts to form. Gradually add 500ml (2 cups) water, stirring, until caramel is dissolved. Add lime zest, cinnamon, kaffir lime leaves and lemongrass, bring to the boil, then simmer for 5 minutes.

2 Add coconut cream, consommé, 180ml (3/4 cup) water and the chicken. Bring to the boil, then reduce heat to very low and simmer for 15 minutes or until chicken is cooked through. Remove pan from heat and leave chicken in poaching liquid for 15 minutes.

3 To make vinegar and lime dressing, mix sugar and vinegar in a saucepan and bring to boil. Simmer for 3 minutes until sugar has dissolved and liquid is syrupy. Cool and stir in the remaining ingredients.

4 To make Asian coleslaw, combine all ingredients in a large bowl and season with salt and pepper. Add half the vinegar and lime dressing and toss to combine.

5 Remove chicken from poaching liquid, shred and season with salt and pepper. Strain poaching liquid through a fine sieve, keeping 250ml (1 cup). Put the 250ml poaching liquid in a large saucepan over medium heat and boil for 6 minutes or until reduced by one-quarter. Cool, then stir in lime juice. Add chicken and toss to coat.

6 Combine chicken with coleslaw and divide among bowls. Drizzle with remaining dressing and scatter with a few extra coriander leaves to serve.

CHICKEN CONSOMME is a clear broth made from richly flavoured stock, available from supermarkets.

"This Asian coleslaw was inspired by Kylie Kwong, my culinary hero." Alvin

Fiona & Matthew's WHITE CHOCOLATE MOUSSE WITH BERRY SWIRL & CRUMBLE

Although the blue team's poached chicken was deemed best main course of Curtis Stone's challenge, Fiona and Matthew saved the red team's honour with this mousse dessert. The tartness of the berries cuts beautifully through the sweet white chocolate and crumble.

250g (1²/₃ cups) plain flour
180g cold unsalted butter, chopped
275g (1¼ cups) caster sugar

300g pkt frozen mixed berries, thawed
WHITE CHOCOLATE MOUSSE
375g white chocolate, chopped

3 egg yolks
600ml pouring cream, whisked to soft peaks

1 To make crumble mixture, preheat oven to 200°C and line a large baking tray with baking paper. Put flour and butter in a bowl and rub in, using your fingertips, until mixture resembles breadcrumbs. Stir in 55g (¼ cup) caster sugar. Spread crumb mixture onto the lined tray and bake for 20 minutes or until golden. Cool, then use a knife to divide roughly into 12 portions and set aside.

2 To make white chocolate mousse, fill a small saucepan one-third full with water and bring to a gentle simmer. Place the chocolate in a heatproof bowl, place over pan and stir until chocolate has melted (don't let the bowl touch the water). Remove bowl from heat and leave for 5 minutes to cool slightly. Whisk in the egg yolks and 2 tbs warm water. Continue whisking until smooth. Fold in the whipped cream in 2 batches and set aside.

3 Combine 110g (½ cup) of the caster sugar and 125ml (½ cup) water in a small saucepan and stir over low heat without boiling until sugar has dissolved. Bring to the boil and cook for 4 minutes until reduced to about 125ml (½ cup). Place berries in a heatproof bowl and pour in syrup. Leave to cool.

4 To make praline, line a large baking tray with foil. Sprinkle remaining caster sugar into a large saucepan and place over medium heat without stirring for 10 minutes or until a caramel forms. Pour onto an oven tray lined with foil and leave for 5 minutes to set. Break into shards and grind to small crystals in a small food processor.

5 To assemble, spoon 2 tbs white chocolate mousse into each of 6 martini glasses (or other 250ml/ 1-cup glasses). Top with 2 tbs berry mixture. Crush 1 portion of the crumble mixture over the top, then add 2 tbs mousse, 2 tbs berries, another portion of crumble, and finish with remaining mousse. Sprinkle with praline* and serve.

STORE any leftover praline in an airtight container at room temperature.

Makes **4**
Preparation **30 minutes**
+ 45 minutes proving
Cooking **25 minutes**

Fiona's BLUE CHEESE & PEAR PIZZA

There were lots of good ideas in this mystery box, but only one pizza was "supreme". Fiona was a mother's dinnertime nightmare as a child, hiding vegetables or giving them to her sisters, and eating only bland food. Now she was triumphant with this great combination of strong flavours: salty prosciutto, creamy, pungent blue cheese and crisp slices of fresh pear.

2 tbs olive oil	6 slices prosciutto, torn	PIZZA DOUGH
4 red onions, sliced	2 pears, sliced	7g sachet dried yeast
2 tbs balsamic vinegar	35g (⅓ cup) walnuts	1 tsp caster sugar
1 tbs sugar	1 bunch rocket	1 pinch salt
Semolina, to sprinkle	Extra virgin olive oil,	300g (2 cups) plain flour
160g creamy blue cheese	to drizzle	2 tbs olive oil

1 To make pizza dough, combine yeast, sugar and salt with 180ml (¾ cup) lukewarm water in a small jug. Leave for 10 minutes until frothy. Place the flour in a large bowl and make a well in the centre. Add the yeast mixture and oil, mix with a wooden spoon and then with hands to make a soft dough.

2 Turn out onto a lightly floured surface and knead for 5 minutes or until smooth and elastic. Place in a lightly oiled bowl, cover with a clean tea towel and leave in a warm place to prove for 45 minutes or until doubled in size.

3 Meanwhile, heat oil in a large frying pan and cook onions over low–medium heat for 15 minutes, stirring occasionally, or until very soft and caramelised. Stir in vinegar and sugar and season to taste. Set aside to cool slightly.

4 Preheat oven to 240°C. Knock down the dough with one firm punch and divide into 4 portions. Roll out on a lightly floured surface to 20cm round. Sprinkle oven trays with semolina and place pizza bases on trays (depending on how many trays you have and size of your oven, you may need to cook pizzas in batches). Spread with caramelised onion, crumble blue cheese over and arrange prosciutto and pears on top. Sprinkle with walnuts.

5 Bake for 10 minutes or until base is crisp underneath. Serve topped with rocket leaves and drizzled with extra virgin olive oil.

Since leaving the competition, Fiona has combined her love of food with her love of teaching and is involved in Stephanie Alexander's Kitchen Garden Foundation.

Makes **4**
Preparation **30 minutes**
+ 45 minutes proving
Cooking **10 minutes**

Sharnee's FIG & PROSCIUTTO PIZZA

"I was really excited to see the ovens because pizza is such a fun dish to make! Often in my family we'll make the bases and prepare the toppings, then everyone creates their own pizza to share. This recipe uses four very rich cheeses that are lightened by the sweet fig and salty prosciutto. The taleggio works particularly well because it oozes so beautifully!"

1 tbs olive oil

2 large red onions, cut into thin wedges

2 cloves garlic, sliced

200ml red wine

1 tbs chopped rosemary

¼ cup oregano leaves

4 figs, cut into thin wedges

12 slices proscuitto, torn into strips

100g grated gruyère

40g (⅓ cup) grated pecorino romano, plus extra to finish

100g taleggio,* sliced

100g buffalo mozzarella,* torn

Extra virgin olive oil, to drizzle

PIZZA DOUGH

7g sachet dried yeast

1 tsp caster sugar

1 pinch salt

300g (2 cups) plain flour

2 tbs olive oil

Semolina, to sprinkle

1 To make pizza dough, combine yeast, sugar and salt with 180ml (¾ cup) lukewarm water in a small jug. Leave for 10 minutes until frothy. Place the flour in a large bowl and make a well in the centre. Add the yeast mixture and oil, mix with a wooden spoon and then with hands to make a soft dough.

2 Turn out onto a lightly floured surface and knead for 5 minutes or until smooth and elastic. Place in a lightly oiled bowl, cover with a clean tea towel and leave in a warm place to prove for 45 minutes or until doubled in size.

3 Meanwhile, heat olive oil in a frying pan and cook onion and garlic over low heat for 20 minutes until soft. Add wine and herbs and cook for 8 minutes or until wine has evaporated. Season to taste. Cool.

4 Preheat oven to 240°C. Knock down the dough with one firm punch and divide into 4 portions. Roll out on a lightly floured surface to make four 20cm rounds. Sprinkle oven trays with semolina and place pizza bases on trays (depending on how many trays you have and size of your oven, you may need to cook pizzas in batches). Spread with the onion mixture and arrange the fig wedges and prosciutto on top. Sprinkle with grated cheeses and scatter with taleggio and mozzarella.

5 Bake for 10 minutes or until base is crisp underneath. Serve sprinkled with extra pecorino, drizzled with extra virgin olive oil and seasoned with salt and freshly ground black pepper.

THESE FOUR CHEESES are traditional, but you can use any varieties you like. Taleggio is an Italian washed-rind cheese and, with buffalo mozzarella and pecorino romano, is available from good delis or specialist cheese shops.

Serves **4**
Preparation **25 minutes**
+ 2 hours freezing
Cooking **10 minutes**

Marion's MANGO & LYCHEE STACKS WITH COCONUT GRANITA

For the tropical fruit invention test Marion wanted to reflect on childhood memories of shopping with her mother at Darwin's eclectic food markets. "You can see and smell dozens of tropical fruits and watch skilled Thai ladies making papaya salad to order. I used fish sauce and chilli with the tropical fruits to re-create that market experience."

2 large mangoes,* peeled, cut
   into cheeks
8 lychees,* seeded, quartered
2 star fruit,* thinly sliced
1/4 cup mint leaves
COCONUT GRANITA
400ml can coconut milk
55g (1/4 cup) caster sugar

FISH SAUCE SYRUP
90g (1/3 cup) grated palm sugar*
1 tsp fish sauce
1/2 lime, juiced
PANKO BREADCRUMB PRALINE
55g (1/4 cup) caster sugar
20g (1/4 cup) Japanese panko
   breadcrumbs*

CHILLI SUGAR
1/2 long red chilli, seeded, finely
   chopped
55g (1/4 cup) caster sugar

1 To make coconut granita, combine coconut milk and sugar in a small saucepan and stir over low heat until sugar dissolves. Place pan over a large bowl filled with ice to cool (or refrigerate, stirring occasionally, until cool). Pour into a 20 x 30cm tray and freeze for 2 hours or until frozen, scraping with a fork every 30 minutes to break up ice crystals.

2 To make fish sauce syrup, combine sugar and 1 tbs water in a saucepan and stir over medium heat for 3 minutes or until sugar dissolves. Simmer for 3 minutes or until syrupy. Stir in fish sauce and lime juice. Set aside until needed.

3 To make panko breadcrumb praline, place sugar in a small pan over medium–high heat and cook, without stirring, until a dark caramel. Meanwhile, sprinkle breadcrumbs over an oven tray lined with baking paper. Pour caramel over breadcrumbs and leave for 10 minutes or until hard. Break into small pieces, then finely chop in a food processor.

4 To make chilli sugar, place chilli, sugar and 1 tsp salt in a bowl. Rub mixture with your fingers to combine (don't overwork or it will become wet).

5 Place mango cheeks, cut-side down, on a work surface and cut each cheek horizontally into two 5mm-thick slices. Using a 6cm round cutter, cut a round from each slice to make 8 rounds.

6 To assemble stacks, place a 6cm ring mould on a plate. Place a mango slice on the bottom, then top with one-quarter of lychees and another mango slice. Press lightly to pack. Remove mould. Repeat with remaining mango and lychees to make 4 stacks. Top with star fruit and scatter with mint. Drizzle with syrup, scatter with panko breadcrumb praline and serve with coconut granita and chilli sugar.

USE FRESH RIPE MANGOES AND LYCHEES when in season and frozen mangoes and canned lychees when out of season. **STAR FRUIT** are sold at Asian grocers and greengrocers. **PALM SUGAR AND JAPANESE PANKO BREADCRUMBS** can be found in the Asian section of selected supermarkets or Asian grocers.

"Sometimes the craziest ideas just seem to work!" Marion

Sharnee's FRUIT MERINGUES WITH GINGER ICE-CREAM & WILD LIME SYRUP

This dessert of meringues, tropical fruit and a few quirky sides is typical of Sharnee's style. "I love to serve food that people can construct themselves. Sweet-tooths can have more macadamia caramel; those who like extra tang could add more wild lime syrup."

Sliced tropical fruit, such as
   mango, lychee and starfruit
MERINGUES
2 egg whites
110g (1/2 cup) caster sugar
1 tsp cornflour
1 tsp white vinegar
GINGER ICE-CREAM
600ml pouring cream
4cm piece ginger, peeled, sliced

1 vanilla bean, split
6 egg yolks
110g (1/2 cup) caster sugar
WILD LIME SYRUP
330g (1 1/2 cups) caster sugar
1/4 cup chopped wild limes*
1/2 vanilla bean, split
MACADAMIA CARAMEL
220g (1 cup firmly packed)
   brown sugar

125ml (1/2 cup) pouring cream
1/4 cup roasted macadamias,
   chopped
VANILLA CREAM
300ml thickened cream
1/2 vanilla bean, split, seeds
   scraped
2 tsp caster sugar

1 To make meringues, preheat oven to 140°C and line 2 large baking trays with baking paper. Use an electric mixer to whisk egg whites to stiff peaks, then gradually add sugar, whisking until thick and glossy. Whisk in the cornflour and vinegar. Scoop 8 large spoonfuls of the mixture and, using another large spoon, drop onto lined trays, leaving 6cm between each. Bake for 15 minutes, then reduce oven to 90°C and bake for a further 30 minutes. Turn off oven and leave inside to cool completely.

2 To make ginger ice-cream, combine cream, ginger and vanilla bean in a saucepan and place over low–medium heat until just below boiling point. Meanwhile, whisk egg yolks and sugar in a heatproof bowl until thick and pale. Gradually add hot cream, whisking continuously. Discard ginger and vanilla bean. Place into a clean saucepan and stir over low heat without boiling for 10 minutes or until mixture thickens to a custard that will coat the back of a spoon.*

3 Strain into a bowl and place over a larger bowl of ice. Stir until cooled, then transfer to an ice-cream maker and churn for 30 minutes or until smooth and frozen. Freeze for 2 hours until firm.

4 To make wild lime syrup, combine sugar and 125ml (1/2 cup) water in a small saucepan. Stir over low heat without boiling until sugar has dissolved. Add limes, vanilla bean and seeds. Increase the heat to medium–high, bring to the boil and cook for 5 minutes or until reduced and syrupy. Strain.

5 To make macadamia caramel, combine sugar and cream in a small saucepan and stir over medium heat until sugar has dissolved and mixture is smooth. Stir in the macadamias.

6 For vanilla cream, whisk cream, vanilla seeds and sugar with electric beaters until soft peaks form.

7 Place fruit in shallow bowls and top with vanilla cream and a meringue. Place a scoop of ice-cream on the side and top with macadamia caramel. Drizzle the plate with lime syrup.

WILD LIMES are available at specialist greengrocers but may need to be ordered; you can use the more common Tahitian lime instead. **ICE-CREAM** can be served as a ginger custard if you don't have time to churn it.

Skye's MANGO MOUSSE WITH A LYCHEE GLASS BALL

Skye's favourite dishes happen when food meets art. "In the middle of the MasterChef kitchen I proceed to flip a tray of hot toffee upside down. Producers are looking at me wondering what on earth I'm up to. Toffee strands begin to set mid-air and drip onto a tray on the floor. A beautiful intricate ball of toffee begins to form and I breathe a huge sigh of relief as I sculpt my lychee glass ball." Well, they do call it an "invention" test.

3 finger limes, halved, fleshy
   capsules scooped out
1 starfruit, sliced crosswise
MANGO MOUSSE
110g (½ cup) caster sugar
2 large mangoes, chopped

3 tsp lime juice
2 x 5g leaves titanium-strength
   gelatine
400ml thickened cream,
   whipped to soft peaks

LYCHEE GLASS BALL
200ml glucose syrup
220g (1 cup) caster sugar
6 lychees, peeled and pitted

1 To make mango mousse, put sugar in a small saucepan with 50ml water. Stir over low heat without boiling until sugar has dissolved. Bring to the boil, then set aside to cool. Reserve 1 tbs of the syrup. Place mango flesh, lime juice and remaining sugar syrup into a blender and purée until smooth.

2 Soak the gelatine leaves in a small bowl of cold water for 5 minutes. Place 125ml (½ cup) of the mango purée into a small saucepan. Squeeze excess liquid from the gelatine and add to pan. Heat gently until gelatine has dissolved. Combine gelatine mixture with remaining mango purée. Cool. Using a large metal spoon, fold in the cream. Spoon into six 185ml (¾-cup) ramekins, moulds or glasses and refrigerate for 4 hours to set.

3 To make the lychee glass balls, combine the glucose syrup, sugar and 50ml water in a small saucepan. Stir over low–medium heat until the sugar has dissolved, then increase the heat to high. Cook for 15 minutes or until the toffee is a pale straw colour. Pour half the toffee onto an oven tray and set aside for 1 minute to cool slightly. Sit the saucepan in a large heatproof bowl of hot water to keep the remaining toffee pliable.

4 Line another oven tray with baking paper and place on the kitchen floor. Hold the toffee tray upside-down over the lower tray so that strands of toffee run onto lower tray. Working quickly, gather the toffee strands and shape into 3 balls, leaving a hole in each to insert the lychee. Repeat to make 6 balls in total. Leave on a sheet of baking paper until needed.

5 To serve, place 2 slices of starfruit onto each plate and top with a little finger lime flesh. Drizzle with reserved sugar syrup. Spoon on the mango mousse and a little more finger lime flesh. Place the lychees inside the balls and add to the plates. Serve immediately.

GLASS BALLS can be made up to 1 hour in advance, though they will start to droop if the weather is humid.

Stephanie Alexander

Stephanie Alexander OAM is the well-known former restaurateur, food writer and champion of quality and diversity in Australian food. She was owner and chef of award-winning Stephanie's Restaurant in Melbourne's Hawthorn from 1976 to 1997. In 2004 she established the not-for-profit Stephanie Alexander Kitchen Garden Foundation with the aim of delivering fun food education to Australian primary school children.

Although this was an elimination pressure test, Jimmy judged the mood correctly when he said, "I don't want to be in any pressure test, but if you have to be in one, this is it". The three contestants flew to Melbourne to cook Stephanie's duck dinner for her in her own home town. They shopped in Peter's local markets and then raced to the rooftop of The Langham, where Stephanie and the judges waited. Timing was all-important... A perfectly poached duck sausage, sliced duck breast and glossy cherry sauce all had to be on the plate when the clock struck twelve.

Peter puts his home-town advantage to good use. Jimmy's plan is to keep him in sight at the market, but Peter disappears into the crowd, leaving Jimmy like a "mouse in a maze".

Serves **6**
Preparation **1 hour**
Cooking **50 minutes**

DUCK DINNER

1 x 2kg duck, neck attached
4 duck breast fillets
1 tbs olive oil
1 onion, roughly chopped
1 carrot, roughly chopped
1 stalk celery, roughly chopped
1 small bulb garlic, halved
6 thyme sprigs
2 bay leaves
2 parsley stalks

1kg duck fat
250g pork mince
100g minced pork fat
70g (½ cup) shelled pistachios, chopped
2 tsp cognac
1 tsp finely grated lemon zest
2 tsp plain flour
1 tbs balsamic vinegar
125ml (½ cup) red wine

500ml (2 cups) chicken stock
1 desiree potato, peeled, very thinly sliced
50g (¼ cup) sour cherries
20g unsalted butter
1 bunch spinach, washed
Mesclun and extra virgin olive oil, to serve

1 Preheat oven to 220°C. Remove neck from duck body and push neck out of skin (it will be attached with little fibres, which should pull off easily). Remove windpipe from skin and discard. Wash skin thoroughly inside and out and set aside.

2 Place duck on a board, breast-side up. To remove legs, pull each leg out from body and cut through skin between body and either side of thigh. Bend whole leg firmly away from body until ball of thigh bone pops from hip socket. Cut between ball and socket to separate leg **(PIC 1)**.
  • Remove skin from both legs and discard. Cut meat from legs and roughly chop. Set aside.

3 Cut along breast bone and against rib cage to remove breasts **(PIC 2)**. Score the skin on all the duck breasts and season with salt and pepper. Refrigerate until needed.

4 Roughly chop remaining carcass. Combine olive oil, duck carcass, onion, carrot, celery, garlic and herbs in a heavy-based roasting pan. Roast for 20 minutes or until browned.

5 Meanwhile, heat the duck fat in a small saucepan to 90°C.* Place chopped leg meat in a small food processor and pulse until smooth.
  • Transfer to an electric mixer fitted with a paddle attachment. Add pork mince, pork fat, pistachios, cognac and lemon zest. Season well with salt and pepper. Mix on medium speed for 3 minutes or until well combined.

1 **2** **3**

- Place the mixture in a piping bag. Tie the narrow end of the neck skin with kitchen string and pipe the mixture into the open end. Using a needle and kitchen string, loosely stitch the large end of the neck **(PIC 3)**. Place neck sausage into the duck fat and poach gently at 90°C for 30 minutes.

6 Meanwhile, stir the flour and vinegar into the roasting pan and return to the oven for 5 minutes. Take out pan and reduce the oven temperature to 200°C.
- Skim any fat from the surface of the pan and place over high heat. Stir in the wine, scraping the bits from the bottom of the pan. Add chicken stock in 2 batches, stirring well after each addition. Reduce heat to low–medium and simmer for 10 minutes.

7 Remove sausage from duck fat and place on an oven tray. Cook in oven for 15 minutes until golden. Reserve 2 tbs of the duck fat. Toss the potato slices in duck fat and arrange on an oven tray in 1 layer. Roast for 5–10 minutes or until golden brown. Season to taste.

8 Strain the stock mixture and place in freezer for 10 minutes, then use paper towel to remove fat from surface. Pour into a saucepan and cook over medium heat for 5 minutes or until reduced and thickened slightly. Add the cherries and adjust seasoning. Keep warm.

9 Preheat a chargrill over high heat. Cook the duck breast, skin-side down, for 5 minutes, then turn and cook for a further 2 minutes. Transfer to an oven tray and cook in oven for 5 minutes for medium-rare, or cooked to your liking. Transfer to a warm plate, cover loosely with foil and rest for 5 minutes.
- Melt butter in a frying pan and cook spinach over medium–high heat for 2 minutes or until wilted.
- Arrange the spinach on plates and top with a 2cm slice of sausage. Thinly slice the breast and arrange on the plate. Spoon on cherry sauce and scatter with the potato crisps. Serve with mesclun dressed with extra virgin olive oil.

YOU WILL NEED a thermometer to ensure you have the duck fat at the right temperature for poaching the sausage.

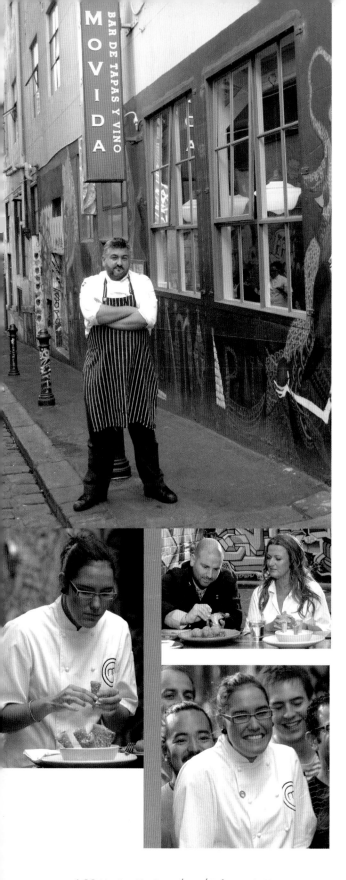

Frank Camorra

MoVida chef and proprietor Frank Camorra was born in Barcelona and spent five years studying architecture before becoming a chef. MoVida embraces the spirit, the fun and the essence of Spain's great bars, while always acknowledging that it sits in the heart of a Melbourne laneway. *The Age Good Food Guide* awarded Camorra Chef of the Year 2009 and MoVida two of its coveted hats.

Marion remembers the challenge to cook Frank's bomba and cornets vividly. "I was terrified and had hardly slept a wink the night before. Cooking in Hosier Lane was an experience in itself, let alone winning the immunity pin. Frank Camorra was so generous with his time and advice during the challenge and extremely gracious in defeat. It was very humbling to meet a chef who has reached such a high level of success and is still willing to encourage and teach an amateur competing against him."

Marion causes a stir in Hosier Lane when she takes on Frank Camorra and beats him at his own bomba.

Makes **16**
Preparation **1 hour**
Cooking **1 hour 10 minutes**

BOMBA

150g (1 cup) plain flour
3 eggs, lightly beaten
100g Japanese panko
   breadcrumbs
Vegetable oil, to deep-fry
MOJO PICON SAUCE
2 large red capsicums
250ml (1 cup) olive oil
1 tbs cumin seeds
1 tbs fennel seeds
1½ tbs sweet paprika

½ tsp hot paprika
100ml sherry vinegar
½ clove garlic, chopped
POTATO CROQUETTES
5 x 200g desiree potatoes
1 tbs olive oil
CHORIZO FILLING
2 tsp olive oil
¼ onion, finely diced
1 chorizo sausage (125g), peeled,
   crumbled

75ml Fino sherry
1 good pinch sweet paprika
1 small pinch hot paprika
BRAVA SAUCE
1 clove garlic
1 egg yolk
2 tsp Dijon mustard
80ml (⅓ cup) sunflower oil
1 tbs lemon juice
60ml (¼ cup) tomato sauce
Tabasco sauce, to taste

1 To make mojo picon sauce, preheat oven to 170°C. Put capsicums in a small roasting pan. Drizzle
with 1 tbs of the olive oil and sprinkle with sea salt. Roast for 45 minutes or until blistered.
- Transfer to a bowl, cover with plastic wrap and leave for 20 minutes, or until cool enough to
handle. Remove the skin, membrane and seeds and roughly chop flesh.
- Meanwhile, roast cumin in a dry frying pan over medium–high heat for 1 minute or until fragrant.
Cool slightly. Using a mortar and pestle, grind cumin very finely and strain through a fine sieve.
Repeat with fennel seeds.
- Mix capsicum in a food processor with ground cumin and fennel. Add the sweet and hot paprikas,
vinegar, garlic and remaining oil. Purée until smooth.

2 To make potato croquettes, put potatoes in a large saucepan and cover with cold water. Bring to the
boil and cook for 25 minutes or until tender. Drain and peel off skin. Push through a potato ricer into
a bowl **(PIC 1)**. Add the olive oil and season to taste. Set aside.

3 To make chorizo filling, heat oil in a frying pan over medium heat and cook onion for 5 minutes or
until soft and translucent. Add chorizo and cook for 5 minutes or until browned. Add sherry, bring to
a simmer and cook for 1 minute. Add sweet and hot paprika and cook until sherry has evaporated.

Mojo picon sauce is a traditional Spanish red capsicum sauce that can also be served as an accompaniment to grilled meat.

- Cool slightly, then chop coarsely in a food processor. Transfer to a bowl and put in fridge to cool.
4 **To make brava sauce,** chop garlic with a pinch of sea salt and crush to a smooth paste. Whisk the garlic paste, egg yolk and mustard until well combined. Whisking continuously, gradually add the oil, a drop at a time at first, then in a thin stream, until thick and emulsified **(PIC 2)**. Whisk in the lemon juice, tomato sauce and Tabasco and season with sea salt.
5 Roll 2 heaped tbs of the potato into a ball. Using your index finger, make a small hole in the potato. Fill with 1 tsp of the cooled chorizo filling **(PIC 3)**. Close the potato mixture around the filling **(PIC 4)** and shape into a smooth ball. Repeat with remaining potato and filling.
6 Coat potato balls in seasoned flour and shake off excess. Dip in egg, allowing excess to drain off. Coat well in the panko. Place onto a large plate or tray and refrigerate until ready to cook.
7 **To cook,** fill a deep fryer or saucepan one-third full with vegetable oil and heat over medium heat to 180°C (or until a cube of bread turns golden in 10 seconds). Cook bomba in batches for 4 minutes or until crisp and golden. Remove with a slotted spoon and drain on paper towel. Season with salt.
8 **To serve,** place a small amount of brava sauce onto serving plates and place bomba on top. Drizzle with more brava sauce and top with a little mojo picon. Serve any remaining sauce on the side.

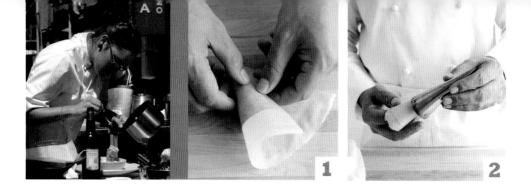

Makes **12**
Preparation **1 hour**
Cooking **45 minutes**

CORNETS WITH CHICKEN LIVER PATE

300g chicken livers
½ small onion, thinly sliced
1 tsp extra virgin olive oil
¼ tsp thyme leaves
360ml Pedro Ximénez sherry*

110g (½ cup) caster sugar
60ml (¼ cup) thickened cream
40g unsalted butter, softened
1 large sheet brik pastry*
1 egg, lightly beaten

1 egg white
300g kikos (roasted corn), finely
  ground*
Uncooked rice, to serve

1 **To make chicken liver pâté,** preheat oven to 170°C. Place the chicken livers in a small roasting pan with the onion, olive oil, thyme and a pinch of salt and mix together. Roast, stirring occasionally, for 12 minutes or until chicken livers are cooked through but still slightly pink in the middle. Remove from the oven and cool slightly.
   • Meanwhile, place 300ml of the sherry and the caster sugar in a small heavy-based saucepan and stir over low heat without boiling until the sugar has dissolved. Bring to the boil, then reduce heat to low. Simmer for 20 minutes or until reduced by one-third. Remove from the heat and leave to cool.
   • Place cooled chicken liver mixture in a food processor. Add cream, butter and remaining sherry, season to taste and process until smooth. Push the mixture through a fine sieve into a bowl. Cover with plastic wrap and place in fridge for 30 minutes or until cool but soft enough to pipe.
2 **To make the cornets,** lay the pastry sheets on a chopping board and cut into 12 even triangles. Roll 1 triangle around a greased metal cone (cream horn mould) **(PIC 1)**. Brush the edge with beaten egg and press together to seal. Slide another cone over the pastry **(PIC 2)**.
   • Place onto the tray and bake for 3–5 minutes or until golden. Remove outer cones and cool on a wire rack. Do this in batches, depending on how many cones you have.
3 Lightly brush the cones with egg white, place back onto the tray and dust with the kikos. Bake again for 1 minute. Cool on a wire rack before removing from the moulds.
4 **To assemble,** drizzle a little sherry syrup on the inside of each cone. Generously pipe the paté into the cones, using a 5mm star nozzle. Drizzle more syrup over the top. Dust with more kikos. Place uncooked rice in a bowl and arrange the cones upright in the rice. Serve immediately.

PEDRO XIMENEZ is a dark, syrupy sherry, available from bottle shops. **BRIK PASTRY** is a Tunisian pastry similar to filo, but slightly thicker. You can buy it from specialist food shops or Middle Eastern food shops. **KIKOS** are roasted corn kernels, sold as 'corn nuts' in nut shops and some supermarkets. Frank uses barbecue flavour.

Chapter Four

SOME DISGUSTINGLY GOOD DISHES

There is open-mouthed horror as Matt Preston smashes Aaron's plate of pasta onto the floor. The mystery box is meaty, a panel of committed carnivores enjoys vegetarian curry, and the first Australian MasterChef pops in for a chat. An Aussie icon inspires some modern cuisine, a Qantas airbus needs refuelling, and George's carrot cake sends Matthew home.

Aaron's PRAWN & FENNEL RAVIOLI WITH CHIPOTLE CHILLI OIL

Matt Preston had a lot of fun with Aaron's risky but fabulous flavours in this invention test, and possibly took a few years off Aaron's life. His eyes blazed as he took the first bite. "That's disgusting," he said, and smashed the plate. The entire set watched in horror...

24 medium green king prawns
1 lemon, zested, juiced
¼ cup chopped flat-leaf parsley
1 bulb baby fennel, trimmed, finely chopped, trimmings reserved
125ml (½ cup) white truffle oil*

80ml (⅓ cup) extra virgin olive oil
1 red onion, finely chopped
2 cloves garlic, thickly sliced
3 tsp ground chipotle chilli*
500g black mussels, scrubbed, beards removed

Salmon roe* and small coriander leaves, to serve
PASTA DOUGH
300g (2 cups) '00' pasta flour*
12 egg yolks
2 tsp olive oil

1 To make pasta, mound flour on work surface, make a well in centre and add yolks, oil and 2 tbs cold water. Draw in flour with a fork until mixture is thick; work in remaining flour with hands. Knead for 6 minutes or until firm; add extra flour if sticky. Wrap in plastic wrap and leave for 20 minutes.

2 To make prawn filling, peel and devein prawns, keeping heads and shells. Finely chop 16 prawns and put in a bowl. Add lemon zest and 1 tbs lemon juice, parsley, fennel and 1 tbs truffle oil to chopped prawns and mix well. Season with salt and pepper. Cut remaining prawns in half lengthwise.

3 To make chipotle chilli oil, heat remaining 105ml truffle oil and 60ml (¼ cup) olive oil over high heat. Add onion and garlic and cook, stirring, for 4 minutes or until onion softens. Add chilli, mussels, remaining lemon juice, fennel trimmings, prawn heads and shells and cook for a further 5 minutes or until mussels open. Reduce heat and simmer gently for 20 minutes. Strain through a fine sieve.

4 Meanwhile, divide pasta dough in 2 and wrap 1 piece in plastic wrap to prevent it drying out. Using a rolling pin, roll out 1 piece until 3mm thick and 12cm wide (nearly the width of a pasta machine). Set machine at its thickest setting (one), then feed the dough through, narrowing the settings on your machine one notch at a time until you reach the thinnest setting (six). Repeat with remaining dough.

5 To make ravioli, place pasta sheets on a lightly floured surface. Place heaped tablespoons of filling, 6cm apart, 3cm up from the bottom of the sheet. Brush around the filling with water, then fold the sheets in half lengthwise to enclose filling. Press gently between filling to remove air pockets. Using a 7cm fluted round cutter, cut out rounds (makes 12) and place on a clean tea towel. Cook ravioli, in 2 batches, in a large saucepan of boiling salted water for 6 minutes. Remove with a slotted spoon, put in a large bowl and toss gently with 2 tbs chipotle chilli oil.

6 Meanwhile, heat remaining olive oil in a large frying pan over high heat and cook halved prawns, stirring, for 2 minutes or until just cooked. Season.

7 Serve ravioli with a little extra chipotle chilli oil, topped with prawns, salmon roe and coriander.

WHITE TRUFFLE OIL is available from specialist food shops. **CHIPOTLE CHILLIES** are smoke-dried jalapeños available from Herbie's Spices in Sydney or by mail order (herbies.com.au) or substitute smoked paprika. **SALMON ROE** is from delis, fishmongers and specialist food shops. **'00' FLOUR,** from supermarkets, is extra-refined flour used to make pasta.

"That's disgusting... Disgustingly good!" Matt Preston

Sharnee's FETTUCCINE WITH GARLIC PRAWNS & LEMON CREME FRAICHE

Sharnee had never made pasta from scratch, so she was very nervous but determined to get it right and keep the sauce light. "This dish showcases the main ingredients: fresh pasta is wonderful dressed with only a little olive oil, verjuice and lemon, as are the prawns. Crème fraîche adds a layer of creamy decadence, complemented by salty bursts of flavour from the capers. George described this as 'elegant', which is exactly what I was hoping for."

12 medium green king prawns,
   peeled, deveined
2 lemons, zested, juiced
4 cloves garlic, crushed
125ml (½ cup) white wine

125ml (½ cup) verjuice*
1 tbs olive oil
120g (½ cup) crème fraîche
Extra lemon zest and micro
   herbs, to serve

PASTA DOUGH
200g '00' pasta flour*
2 eggs
2 tsp olive oil

1 To make pasta dough, process flour, eggs and olive oil with a good pinch of salt in a food processor until mixture comes together. Turn out onto a lightly floured work surface and knead for 5 minutes or until smooth. Wrap in plastic wrap and leave at room temperature for 20 minutes.

2 Divide pasta dough in 2 and wrap 1 piece in plastic wrap to prevent it drying out. Using a rolling pin, roll out 1 piece until 3mm thick and 12cm wide (nearly the width of a pasta machine). Set machine at its thickest setting (one), then feed the dough through, narrowing the settings on your machine one notch at a time until you reach the thinnest setting (six). Repeat with remaining dough.

3 Cut each pasta sheet in half. Using the fettuccine cutter on the pasta machine, feed the dough through. Hang fettuccine over the back of a chair or a clean clothes drying rack for 10 minutes to dry.

4 Meanwhile, toss prawns with lemon zest and garlic and marinate in the fridge for 15 minutes.

5 Combine white wine, verjuice, lemon juice and olive oil in a frying pan. Bring just to the boil, reduce heat to low and simmer over medium heat for 2 minutes or until slightly reduced. Add the prawns and cook, turning occasionally, until changed colour and cooked through.

6 Cook fettuccine in a large saucepan of boiling salted water for 2 minutes or until al dente. Drain and toss with the sauce. Serve with a dollop of crème fraîche, topped with extra lemon zest and herbs.

VERJUICE is unripe grape juice and is used in similar ways to lemon juice or vinegar. It's available from supermarkets and delis or use white wine vinegar instead. **'00' FLOUR,** from supermarkets, is extra-refined flour used to make pasta.

HANG FETTUCCINE over the back of a chair or on a clean drying rack, so that the strands don't tangle while it dries after rolling and cutting.

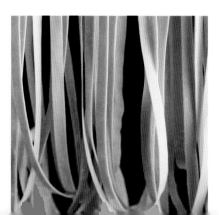

Maggie Beer

Maggie Beer turned a simple farm shop into Australia's best restaurant. The Barossa legend, creative head of Maggie Beer Farm Shop and Products, cook and TV presenter, challenged Aaron to a pie bake. Maggie's food philosophy is simple: fresh ingredients, sourced as close to home as possible.

   As the prize for winning the pasta invention test, Aaron had the honour of cooking Maggie's **pheasant pie with radicchio and black pig bacon braise.** "It doesn't get much better than that! She was one of the warmest, most generous and friendly people I have ever met. Even though I had a bad day in the kitchen, for me it was not about winning or losing – it was about a once-in-a-lifetime experience. Cooking with Maggie Beer... who else gets to do that?"

"You'll be fine, because I'm every bit as nervous as you are." Maggie and Aaron face off in the most delicious pie bake ever.

Serves **6-8**
Preparation 1½ **hours**
Cooking 1½ **hours**

PHEASANT PIE WITH BRAISED RADICCHIO & BLACK PIG BACON BRAISE

1.2kg pheasant
60ml (¼ cup) verjuice*
MARINADE
125ml (½ cup) olive oil
1 orange, zest pared into strips, juiced
8 thyme sprigs
4 bay leaves
1 tbs crushed juniper berries
SOUR CREAM PASTRY
200g unsalted butter, chilled
250g (1⅔ cups) plain flour
135g sour cream
PIE FILLING
60g butter

2 cloves garlic, finely chopped
1 tbs chopped rosemary
350g portobello mushrooms, sliced
Extra virgin olive oil, to fry
30g plain flour
250ml (1 cup) chicken stock
2 tbs crème fraîche
40g walnuts, roasted, skins rubbed off
1 lemon, zested
2 tbs chopped oregano
GLAZE
1 egg yolk
2 tsp milk

BRAISED RADICCHIO
125g radicchio
1½ tbs currants
2 tbs verjuice
50g black pig or free-range bacon, cut into 2cm pieces
2 tbs extra virgin olive oil
1 tsp rosemary, finely chopped
1 tbs vino cotto,* or more to taste
¼ cup parsley, roughly chopped
PHEASANT JUS
750ml (3 cups) chicken stock
1 tbs verjuice

1 To prepare pheasant, cut off end of wings with a sharp knife **(PIC 1)**. To remove the legs, pull one leg out from the body and cut through the skin between the body and both sides of the thigh **(PIC 2)**. Bend the whole leg firmly away from the body, until the ball of the thigh bone pops from the hip socket. Cut between the ball and the socket to separate the leg. Repeat to remove the other leg.
• Combine marinade ingredients in a large shallow dish. Add pheasant legs and body and turn to coat. Marinate in the fridge for at least 10 minutes.

2 To make sour cream pastry, pulse butter and flour in a food processor until it resembles coarse breadcrumbs. Add sour cream and pulse until the dough starts to come together in a ball. Turn out and shape pastry into a rectangle with your hands. Wrap in plastic and refrigerate for 10 minutes.
• Roll out the pastry on a lightly floured surface to 3mm thick. Cut a 28cm round of pastry for the pie base and a 23cm round for the top. Line a 23cm pie dish with the larger piece of pastry. Place the other piece onto a board and place in the fridge to rest until required.

3 To roast pheasant, preheat oven to 220°C. Season pheasant well. Place on an oven tray, skin-side up. Roast for 10 minutes, then turn pieces over. The legs will need a further 10 minutes roasting, and the breast a further 20 minutes. If unsure, poke a skewer into the thickest part of the breast to check the juices run clear. When legs have been removed from the oven, splash with half the verjuice. When breast is removed from oven, place upside down in roasting pan with legs and splash with remaining verjuice. Rest for 15 minutes until cool enough to handle. Increase the oven to 230°C.

 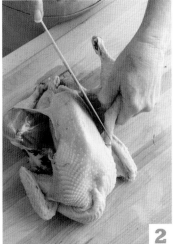 

4 To make pie filling, heat butter in a frying pan over high heat. Fry garlic and rosemary, then add mushrooms. Cook for 8 minutes or until mushrooms are soft and reduced by half, adding a little extra virgin olive oil if necessary. Season with 1 tsp salt while cooking.

   • Add the flour to the pan and stir over heat for 3 minutes. Stir in chicken stock and bring to the boil. Stir in crème fraîche and reduce heat to a simmer. Cook for 5 minutes or until thickened. Season and then leave in fridge for about 30 minutes to cool completely.

5 To bone pheasants, separate drumsticks from thighs and remove bones from thighs **(PIC 3)**. To remove breast meat, cut away by following the carcass down to the wing joint. Slice off the plump pieces of meat. Carve breast and leg into bite-sized pieces. If the orange zest in the pheasant has not burned, chop and fold with the meat, walnuts, lemon zest and oregano into pie filling mixture.

6 To cook pie, make a glaze by whisking egg yolk and milk with a good pinch of salt. Take pastry from the fridge and spoon pheasant filling into dish. Cover with pastry top, crimp and seal edges. Brush with glaze and score with a pattern if liked. If pastry warms too much, return to fridge for 5 minutes.

   • Bake the pie for 5 minutes, then reduce oven to 220°C and cook for a further 25 minutes or until pastry is golden and cooked through.*

7 To make braised radicchio, trim radicchio stems and cut leaves into 2cm slices. Place currants and verjuice in a small saucepan and bring to a simmer, then remove from heat and set aside.

   • Heat a non-stick frying pan over medium heat. Cook the bacon in the dry pan for 5 minutes until crisp. Remove bacon and set aside. Add the oil to the pan and cook the rosemary for 1 minute. Add radicchio, season with salt and cook for 4 minutes or until radicchio has wilted.

   • Add the currants and verjuice and reduce to low heat. Cook for a few minutes. Add the vino cotto and cook for 2 minutes or until syrupy. Stir in chopped parsley and return the bacon to the pan. Check seasoning, set aside and keep warm.

8 To make pheasant jus, add the resting juices from the pheasant to the stock and verjuice in a small saucepan. Cook over medium heat for 15–20 minutes or until reduced to a sauce-like consistency. Strain into a serving jug.

9 Leave pie to rest slightly before cutting. Serve with braised radicchio and pheasant jus.

VERJUICE is unripe grape juice that is used in similar ways to lemon juice or vinegar and is available from specialist food shops. If necessary, use white wine vinegar instead. **VINO COTTO** is a condiment made from cooked grape must. If necessary, use aged balsamic vinegar or a balsamic reduction instead. **FOR EVEN COLOURING** of the pastry top, turn the pie halfway through cooking, if necessary.

Serves **4**
Preparation **35 minutes**
Cooking **30 minutes**

Peter's STEAK & POTATO GALETTE WITH ONION RINGS

For Peter, this meaty mystery box was a great opportunity to turn basic midweek dinner ingredients into something special. "That is quite a familiar challenge for me! What I love about this dish is that, with just a few little tricks, a simple meal of steak and potatoes can transport you to a rustic bistro in the French countryside. What nicer way to end the day?"

4 x 180g scotch fillet steaks
2 tsp red wine vinegar
1½ tbs olive oil
1 tsp Dijon mustard
2 baby cos lettuce
HORSERADISH SALSA
50g fresh horseradish, very finely
  grated

1 tsp Dijon mustard
2 tbs olive oil
2 tsp red wine vinegar
2 tbs finely chopped parsley
POTATO GALETTE
3 desiree potatoes (500g)
  peeled, thinly sliced*
75g clarified butter

ONION RINGS
150g (1 cup) plain flour
180ml (¾ cup) beer,
  approximately
1 onion, peeled,
  sliced into rings
Vegetable oil, to deep-fry

1 To make the horseradish salsa, gently mix all the ingredients in a small bowl.

2 To make the galette, preheat oven to 240°C. Mark four 14cm circles on a sheet of baking paper and place paper, pencil-side down, on a large baking tray. Dry potato slices with paper towel, place in a bowl, season with salt and pepper and toss with clarified butter. Place a slice of potato into the centre of a circle and arrange overlapping slices of potato around it. Repeat to make two layers, then make 3 more rounds with the remaining potato. Bake for 10 minutes or until base is lightly browned. Turn galettes carefully with an egg slice and cook for a further 10 minutes or until brown and crisp.

3 For the onion rings, sift flour and a pinch of salt into a mixing bowl and make a well in the centre. Gradually add the beer, whisking to a smooth batter the consistency of pouring cream (add more or less beer as needed). Fill a deep fryer or large saucepan one-third full with vegetable oil and heat over medium heat to 180°C (or until a cube of bread turns golden in 10 seconds). Working in 4 batches, dip the onion rings into the batter, letting excess batter drain off. Gently drop into the oil and fry, turning halfway, for 3 minutes or until crisp and golden. Remove with a slotted spoon and drain on paper towel. Season with salt.

4 Preheat a large heavy-based frying pan or barbecue plate over medium–high heat. Lightly oil the steaks and cook for 3 minutes each side for medium–rare, or to your liking. Rest for 5 minutes.

5 Combine the vinegar, oil and mustard to make a dressing. To serve, arrange the potato galettes on plates, top with the steaks and spoon a little horseradish salsa on top. Add the onion rings and lettuce leaves, drizzle lettuce with dressing and serve immediately.

IF YOU HAVE A MANDOLIN, use it here to thinly slice the potato.

Serves **4**
Preparation **10 minutes**
Cooking **30 minutes**

Claire's STEAK WITH POTATOES, DIJON BUTTER & CABBAGE SALAD

Claire was happy to be up front for tasting again with this "pub food" dish. What George loved most was the cabbage salad and beautiful Dijon butter. Claire chose very simple ingredients but put up a fantastically flavoursome dish. Matt felt she'd delivered exactly what they hoped to see, including potatoes perfect for soaking up those meat juices.

2 large sebago potatoes (500g), scrubbed

250g cabbage, very finely shredded

1¹/₂ tsp salt

60ml (¹/₄ cup) red wine vinegar

1¹/₂ tbs brown sugar

150g butter, softened

70g (¹/₄ cup) Dijon mustard

60ml (¹/₄ cup) olive oil

4 x 250g sirloin steaks

30g fresh horseradish, very finely grated

1 Preheat oven to 220°C. Cut the potatoes in half lengthwise and place, cut-side down, on a lightly greased oven tray. Bake for 20–25 minutes or until just cooked.

2 Meanwhile, place cabbage in a bowl and sprinkle with salt. Leave for 10 minutes to draw out the moisture, then drain off the liquid. Toss with the vinegar and sugar.

3 To make Dijon butter, mix together butter and mustard, season and refrigerate until needed.

4 Heat 1 tbs oil in a large frying pan (or two smaller frying pans). Season the steaks and cook over high heat for 2 minutes each side. Rest for 5 minutes.

5 To finish the potatoes, press with a potato masher until squashed but still in one piece. Heat the remaining oil in a large frying pan and cook potatoes over medium–high heat for 3 minutes each side or until golden. Sprinkle cut-side with horseradish.

6 Serve steak and potatoes with the pickled cabbage on the side and a little Dijon butter.

Serves **8**
Preparation **45 minutes**
Cooking **50 minutes**

Adam and Aaron's PUMPKIN CURRY WITH GOAT'S CHEESE & SPINACH PARATHAS

For the vegetarian challenge the teams were to be judged by a panel of "burly blokes", all decidedly unconvinced of the joys of a dish without meat. But they loved this curry. Aaron took charge of the bread, while Adam cooked the curry. "When I worked in India, I loved the vegetarian food there. With so much flavour and texture you hardly have time to miss the meat. The salty goat's cheese made this curry. Aaron and I made a last-minute decision to crumble it on top and it perfectly offset the sweetness of the pumpkin and coconut milk. I'm pleased now to have an absolute winner of a vegetarian dish in my repertoire!"

2 tbs cumin seeds

3 tbs coriander seeds

1 tbs black peppercorns

2–3 tsp chilli powder

60ml (¼ cup) vegetable oil

3 large onions, finely diced

5 cloves garlic, finely chopped

750ml (3 cups) coconut milk

1 butternut pumpkin (1.8kg), peeled, cut into 1.5cm cubes

80g baby spinach leaves

100g goat's cheese, crumbled

GOAT'S CHEESE & SPINACH PARATHAS

450g (3 cups) plain flour

80g baby spinach leaves

100g goat's cheese, crumbled

Vegetable oil, to shallow-fry

1 Roast the cumin and coriander seeds in a dry frying pan over medium heat for 2 minutes or until fragrant. Cool. Using a mortar and pestle, finely grind the roasted seeds with the peppercorns in 2 batches. Pass through a sieve to remove any large pieces and combine with the chilli powder.

2 Heat the oil in a wok and cook the onions and garlic over medium heat for 4 minutes or until soft. Stir in the spice mixture. Add the coconut milk and 250ml (1 cup) water and bring to the boil. Reduce the heat to low–medium and simmer for 25 minutes, stirring occasionally. Add pumpkin to the wok and simmer for about 10 minutes or until soft. Add spinach and stir until wilted.

3 To make paratha, put flour in a food processor. With motor running, slowly add 330ml (1⅓ cups) water, processing until mixture begins to clump together. Turn out onto a lightly floured surface and gather together. Knead for 5 minutes until smooth. Wrap in plastic wrap and leave for 10 minutes.

4 Bring a large saucepan of water to the boil and blanch the spinach for a few seconds until wilted. Drain, then refresh in iced water. Drain again and squeeze out the excess water. Chop finely.

5 Divide dough into 8 portions. Use a rolling pin to roll out on a lightly floured surface to 10cm rounds, about 1cm thick. Sprinkle the spinach and cheese over the dough rounds. Roll each round into a cigar shape 14cm long, then curl into a spiral. Use the rolling pin again to roll out to a 16cm round.

6 Heat 1cm oil in a large frying pan and cook parathas in batches for 1½ minutes each side or until puffed and golden. Drain on paper towels. Serve curry, topped with crumbled goat's cheese, with the parathas on the side.

Claire and Jonathan's FRIED FIGS WITH GOAT'S CHEESE

Claire and Jonathan made the brave decision to serve figs to the truckies, builders and other dedicated carnivore judges of the vegetarian challenge (who described their favourite vegetable as "a rump steak"). The panel looked bemused when the platter was brought to the table. "I don't know what they were expecting, but I suspect this wasn't it," remembers Claire. But then they polished off the lot with gusto.

7g sachet dried yeast
55g (¼ cup) sugar
200g (1⅓ cups) plain flour
250ml (1 cup) balsamic vinegar
1 tsp pepperberries*

26 ripe figs
100ml thickened cream
100g soft goat's cheese, at room
   temperature
Sunflower oil, to deep-fry

½ cup walnuts, roasted and
   chopped
1 cup micro herbs or cress

1 Combine the yeast and 1 tbs of the sugar in a large bowl with 100ml lukewarm water and leave for 5 minutes until foamy. Add another 200ml water to the bowl, then gradually add the flour and ¼ tsp salt and whisk until smooth. Set aside to rest for 20 minutes.

2 Mix the balsamic vinegar and pepperberries in a small saucepan and bring to the boil over medium heat. Reduce the heat and simmer for 10 minutes or until reduced and slightly syrupy. Set aside.

3 Peel 10 of the figs and roughly chop the flesh. Combine in a non-stick frying pan with the remaining sugar. Stir over low–medium heat to dissolve the sugar. Cook, stirring occasionally to prevent sticking, for 10 minutes or until the mixture has a jammy consistency.

4 Use an electric mixer to whisk the cream to soft peaks, then whisk the goat's cheese to soften. Fold half the cream into the goat's cheese, then fold in the remaining cream. Season with salt.

5 Fill a deep-fryer or large saucepan one-third full with sunflower oil and heat over medium heat to 180°C (or until a cube of bread turns golden in 10 seconds). Dip the figs into the batter and fry in batches of 3 for 2 minutes or until golden and crisp. Drain on paper towel.

6 To serve, spoon goat's cheese mixture onto each plate and top with fig purée and two fried figs. Drizzle the balsamic reduction around the plate and scatter with walnuts and micro herbs.

PEPPERBERRIES are a native food, available from specialist food shops, or 'bush tucker' or spice suppliers. Use black peppercorns if you can't find pepperberries.

Serves **6**

Preparation **30 minutes**

Cooking **20 minutes**

Marion's LEMON & MINT SPRING ROLLS WITH SYRUP

There was a palpable hum of excitement when MasterChef Julie Goodwin arrived in the kitchens to take her turn on "the other side of the tasting table". The mystery box contained lemon, cream cheese and peanuts, and Marion enjoyed herself with bold flavours and crisp pastry. "I've learned so much from my Thai mum when it comes to cooking, including the technique of making spring roll wrappers from scratch. It's not as hard as it sounds!"

225g (1½ cups) plain flour
250g cream cheese, chopped,
   softened
1 egg yolk

110g (½ cup) caster sugar
4 lemons, zested
2 tbs finely shredded mint leaves
Vegetable oil, to deep-fry

Chopped roasted salted peanuts,
   torn mint leaves and icing
   sugar, to serve

1 To make spring roll wrappers, place flour in bowl. Gradually stir in 250ml (1 cup) cold water to form a sticky paste, adding more flour or water if needed. Cover with plastic wrap and leave for 10 minutes.

2 Heat a 26cm non-stick crêpe pan over low heat until just warm. Spoon 1 heaped tbs of paste into the centre of the pan and, using a small cranked palette knife,* spread quickly and evenly to a 15cm round. Cook for 30 seconds or until edges of wrapper start to curl. Peel off wrapper and place, cooked-side down, on a plate lined with baking paper. Repeat to make 12 wrappers, stacking them on top of each other with baking paper between each layer. Cover the remaining paste with a slightly damp clean tea towel and keep for sealing the spring rolls.

3 Meanwhile, to make filling, using an electric mixer, beat cream cheese, egg yolk, 2 tsp sugar and half lemon zest until pale and fluffy. Stir in mint and spoon into piping bag fitted with a 1.5cm plain nozzle.

4 To make lemon syrup, place remaining 100g sugar and 125ml (½ cup) water in a small saucepan, bring to the boil over high heat, then simmer for 5 minutes or until slightly thick. Remove pan from heat and stir in the remaining lemon zest. Set syrup aside to cool completely.

5 To assemble the spring rolls, place a wrapper, uncooked-side up, on a work surface. Starting 2cm up from the bottom, pipe a 3cm line of filling widthwise across the bottom half of the wrapper. Fold up the bottom of the wrapper over the filling, then fold in the sides and roll up, leaving a small flap. Dab a little reserved paste on flap, then roll up completely to secure spring roll. Transfer, seam-side down, to an oven tray lined with baking paper. Repeat with remaining wrappers and filling.

6 Fill a deep-fryer or large saucepan one-third full with oil and heat over medium heat to 170°C (or until a cube of bread turns golden in 10 seconds). Fry spring rolls in 3 batches for 2 minutes or until golden. Drain on paper towel.

7 Divide spring rolls among plates and drizzle with lemon syrup. Scatter with chopped peanuts and mint, then dust with icing sugar to serve.

A CRANKED PALETTE KNIFE has a blade with a 'step' near the handle, which keeps your hand above and clear of where you're working. If you don't have one, you can use an ordinary palette knife.

"This is a really beautiful dish, and something I would've liked to have had more of... if Matt hadn't taken so much on the first taste."

Julie Goodwin

Serves **4**
Preparation **20 minutes**
Cooking **20 minutes**

Alvin's SEARED LAMB WITH CHILLI & PEANUT CARAMEL

Alvin's mystery box dish was stunning. The flavour combination of perfectly cooked lamb, hot chillies stuffed with cream cheese, plus sweet-and-salty peanut caramel and poached egg was inspired by David Chang from Momofuku in New York, but pulled off in Alvin's own inimitable style.

55g (¼ cup) caster sugar
75g (½ cup) unsalted roasted peanuts
2 bird's-eye chillies, seeded, finely chopped

10 mint leaves, finely chopped
2 tbs lemon juice
4 long red chillies
80g (⅓ cup) cream cheese, chopped, softened

2 tsp vegetable oil
2 lamb backstraps
4 eggs
Small mint leaves, to serve

1 Preheat the oven to 180°C. Combine the sugar with 2 tbs water in a frying pan. Stir over low heat without boiling to dissolve the sugar, then bring to the boil and cook for 4 minutes or until golden. Stir in the peanuts, chopped chillies and mint. Pour onto an oven tray lined with foil and leave for 5 minutes to set. Break into shards and, using a mortar and pestle or food processor, grind to coarse crumbs. Stir in 2 tsp of the lemon juice and set aside.

2 Cut a slit lengthways in each large chilli and scoop out the seeds. Mix the cream cheese with the remaining lemon juice and stuff into the long chillies.

3 Heat the oil in an ovenproof frying pan over medium–high heat and cook the lamb for 2½ minutes on each side for medium–rare. Transfer to the oven and cook for 2½ minutes. Leave to rest for 10 minutes, then cut across the grain into thin slices.

4 Meanwhile, heat 5cm water in a large frying pan until just simmering. Working one at a time, carefully crack the eggs into a cup and slide into the water. Cook gently for 3 minutes or until the whites have set. Remove with a slotted spoon.

5 Serve slices of lamb topped with an egg, a stuffed chilli and some peanut caramel. Scatter with a few small mint leaves.

For many contestants the mystery box was a highlight of the week: a time to go wild (or "wildly creative") and show the judges their personal culinary styles.

Serves **6**
Preparation **20 minutes**
+ 2 hours refrigeration
Cooking **15 minutes**

Sharnee's **LEMON CHEESECAKE MOUSSE WITH SHORTBREAD**

This is quick and easy and can be prepared well in advance. Sharnee says the trick is in the presentation. "Elegant glassware always looks beautiful, and the green of the mint sugar sits well on the pale lemon mousse. Instead of lemon, you could use fresh passionfruit or raspberries. Just strain the fruit through a sieve to remove any seeds. The shortbread adds crunchy, crumbly texture and could be crumbled on top or layered through the mousse."

4 egg yolks
300g (1⅓ cups) caster sugar
500g cream cheese, chopped, softened
2 lemons, zested, 1 juiced

6 egg whites
¼ cup finely shredded mint leaves
SHORTBREAD
105g (¾ cup) plain flour

80g cold unsalted butter, chopped
110g (½ cup) caster sugar
1 egg

1 To make mousse, using an electric mixer, beat egg yolks and 220g (1 cup) sugar until thick and pale. Add cream cheese, lemon zest, and juice of 1 lemon and beat until smooth. In a clean bowl, whisk egg whites to stiff peaks. Fold one-third of egg whites into cheese mixture, then fold in remainder until just combined. Divide mixture among six 375ml (1½-cup) glasses and chill for 2 hours.

2 Meanwhile, to make shortbread, place flour, butter and 55g (¼ cup) sugar in a food processor and process until the mixture resembles breadcrumbs. Add egg and process until the mixture just comes together. Turn out dough onto a lightly floured work surface and form into a disc. Wrap in plastic and refrigerate for 20 minutes.

3 Preheat oven to 200°C. Roll out dough between 2 floured sheets of baking paper until 5mm thick, then refrigerate for 10 minutes. Using a 5cm pastry cutter, cut out 12 rounds and place on an oven tray lined with baking paper. Refrigerate for 10 minutes. Place the remaining 55g (¼ cup) sugar in a bowl and roll the edges of the rounds in sugar. Bake for 12 minutes or until pale golden. Cool for 5 minutes on tray, then transfer to a wire rack to cool completely.

4 To make minted sugar, mix together mint, remaining lemon zest and remaining sugar in a bowl. Scatter over cheesecake mousse and serve with shortbread.

Marion's **WINE BAR ROLLS**

The reward for winning the mystery box is to choose the main ingredient for the invention test. When Marion won the Julie Goodwin mystery box and stepped into the pantry, what awaited her was a little different. No cheese, chicken, mangoes or even goat... The cloths were lifted and the choice was Iced VoVos, Golden Gaytimes or Chiko Rolls. And the theme? Re-making the Aussie food icon.

   Marion chose the Chiko Roll. "This was a tough challenge, especially as I had never tasted a Chiko Roll before – although I wasn't alone! I decided I wanted to keep the spirit of this well-known roll but take it from a footy staple to a dish worthy of a wine bar menu. A lot of technique went into one little roll and I had no idea whether it would be a winner or a disaster. Popping the first roll into the hot oil to deep-fry was certainly a tense moment. I crossed my fingers and hoped the whole thing wouldn't fall apart. The kitchen gods must have been smiling on me that day because, not only did the dish work, but George loved it."

Marion on a roll! She took out the mystery box with her spring rolls and then took on the Chiko Roll in her modern interpretation of an Aussie icon.

Marion's **WINE BAR ROLLS**

Serves **8**
Preparation **45 minutes**
Cooking **1½ hours**

10 cloves garlic, unpeeled
1 tbs soy sauce
1 tbs olive oil
Peanut oil, to deep-fry
6 green beans, thinly sliced
   diagonally, blanched*

BRAISED BEEF

4 cloves garlic, peeled
2 tsp sea salt
300g beef shin, cut into
   2cm cubes
250ml (1 cup) extra virgin
   olive oil
250ml (1 cup) peanut oil

FILLING

3 large coliban potates, peeled,
   cut into 3cm pieces
2 tbs extra virgin olive oil
80g cabbage, very finely
   shredded
2 cloves garlic, thinly sliced
5 green beans, thinly sliced
   diagonally, blanched
2 tsp soy sauce

CREPES

150g (1 cup) plain flour
Butter, to cook
   crêpes

BATTER

150g (1 cup) plain flour
2 eggs, lightly beaten

CABBAGE SALAD

80g cabbage, very finely
   shredded
1 carrot, cut into julienne
   (matchsticks)
1 tbs extra virgin olive oil
1 tsp soy sauce

1 Preheat oven to 150°C. Place the garlic on a small oven tray and bake for 20 minutes or until soft and lightly golden. Set aside to cool, then peel off skin and dress garlic with soy sauce and olive oil.

2 **To make braised beef,** using a mortar and pestle, lightly pound the garlic cloves with the salt. Add to the beef and massage into the meat. Leave to stand for 5 minutes.
  • Combine the oils in a wide ovenproof saucepan and bring to a simmer. Add the meat and stir gently. Cut a round of baking paper and use to cover the meat, pressing down gently. Put pan in oven and bake for 40 minutes or until tender. Lift meat from pan with a slotted spoon. Chop the meat finely and keep the braised garlic.

3 **To make filling,** place the potatoes in a large saucepan and cover with cold salted water. Bring to the boil, then reduce the heat slightly and simmer for 15 minutes or until tender. Drain well then, using a wooden spoon, press the potatoes through a sieve into a bowl **(PIC 1).***
  • Add 1 tbs of the oil to the potatoes and mix well. Heat remaining oil in a small frying pan and add the cabbage, garlic and beans. Cook over medium heat for 2 minutes or until softened. Stir in the soy sauce and season with salt and pepper. Combine the cabbage mixture, beef mixture, mashed potato and braised garlic cloves in a bowl. Mix well and season with pepper.

4 **To make crêpes,** place flour and a pinch of salt in a bowl and make a well in centre. Gradually add 375ml (1½ cups) water, mixing until smooth. Melt a little butter in an 18cm non-stick frying pan or crêpe pan over medium heat. Pour 60ml (¼ cup) batter into pan and swirl to cover base **(PIC 2),** Cook for 1 minute or until lightly browned underneath. Turn over and cook for 1 minute until golden.

For this challenge, Marion very cleverly dissected the flavour of the Chiko Roll and used that as inspiration for a filling for crêpes.

- Transfer cooked crêpe to a plate lined with baking paper. Repeat with the remaining batter, greasing the pan with butter each time, to make 8 crêpes. Keep bowl to one side to use a little leftover batter when assembling the rolls.

5 To make batter, place the flour in a bowl and make a well in the centre. Add the eggs, then gradually add 180ml (3/4 cup) water, mixing to a smooth, thick batter.

6 To assemble rolls, place 1/4 cup of the filling along the centre of each crêpe. Roll up, tucking in the sides as you go **(PIC 3)**. Seal the join with a little reserved crêpe batter.

7 Fill a deep-fryer or large saucepan one-third full with peanut oil and heat over medium heat to 180°C (or until a cube of bread turns golden in 10 seconds). Working in 3 batches, dip rolls into batter, allowing excess to drain off, then gently drop into the oil. Cook, turning a few times, for 4 minutes or until crisp and golden. Remove with a slotted spoon* and drain on paper towel.

8 To serve, toss the cabbage salad ingredients together gently and place 3 small piles onto each plate. Trim the ends of the rolls and cut each into 3 rounds. Place on cabbage salad and top with a little pile of sliced beans. Add the roasted garlic to the plates and dress with soy and oil dressing. Serve immediately, before the crisp batter softens.

TO BLANCH GREEN BEANS cook in boiling water for 3 minutes, then drain and tip into a bowl of iced water to stop the cooking process. Beans should be tender but still crisp. **A WOODEN SPOON AND SIEVE** will give you the same effect as a potato ricer. **USE A SLOTTED SPOON** rather than tongs to lift rolls from hot oil. Tongs could tear the crisp batter.

Jonathan's CLASSIC BEEF STEW WITH CORNMEAL CHIPS

Jonathan, too, had never tasted a Chiko Roll: "I was intrigued to find so many vegetables in it... I had no idea! To 'reinvent' this icon, I decided to use all those beautiful vegies as a feature and then try to create an 'essence of Chiko Roll' that I would serve as the sauce." His dish went on to win the challenge and he cooked off again, against chef Josh Emett.

50g (¼ cup) pearl barley
1 sprig thyme
1 carrot, cut into 1cm cubes
100g green beans, trimmed, cut
    into 5mm pieces
100g cabbage, finely shredded
1 tbs olive oil

400g beef fillet, cut into 1cm
    cubes
1 small onion, finely chopped
SAUCE
1 tbs olive oil
200g beef ribs, cut into pieces
1 small onion, finely chopped

1 carrot, grated
1 sprig parsley
1 sprig thyme
30g cold butter, diced
CORNMEAL CHIPS
60g (½ cup) white cornmeal
Vegetable oil, to shallow–fry

1 Put pearl barley and thyme in a small saucepan with 375ml (1½ cups) water. Bring to the boil over high heat, then reduce heat and simmer, covered, for 35 minutes or until tender; drain. Transfer to a large bowl, season with salt and set aside.

2 To make sauce, heat oil in a frying pan and brown beef ribs over high heat. Remove ribs from pan. Add onion to pan, reduce heat to medium and cook, stirring, for 5 minutes or until browned. Add carrot and cook until lightly browned. Return meat to pan, add parsley, thyme and 500ml (2 cups) water. Bring to the boil, then reduce heat and simmer for 30 minutes or until brown, a little syrupy and reduced by a little more than half.

3 Meanwhile, to make the cornmeal chips, combine the cornmeal and ½ tsp salt in a bowl and make a well in the centre. Add 60ml (¼ cup) water and mix to a dough, adding a little more water if necessary. Knead briefly in the bowl. Divide into 4 portions and roll out each one between 2 sheets of baking paper until 2mm thick. Cut discs with a 10cm cutter. Heat 1cm oil in a frying pan over medium–high heat. Cook the discs for 2 minutes on each side or until crisp and well browned. Drain on paper towel. Transfer to a plate and cover with foil; keep warm in a low oven.

4 Drop the carrot cubes into a saucepan of boiling water and cook for 2 minutes or until just tender. Lift out with a slotted spoon and refresh in cold water, then drain well. Add to pearl barley in bowl. Repeat with the beans, then add the cabbage to the water and cook for 30 seconds. Drain and refresh under cold water. Drain again and add to the bowl.

5 Strain the sauce into a clean pan and add pearl barley and vegetables. Bring to a simmer and cook for a few minutes until slightly reduced. Whisk in butter gradually and season with salt and pepper.

6 Heat the olive oil in a large frying pan over high heat. Add the beef and cook, turning often, until well browned. Remove from the pan and reduce heat to medium. Add onion and cook for 3 minutes or until soft but not coloured. Return beef to pan with the sauce. Warm through and season. Serve topped with a cornmeal chip.

Makes **8**
Preparation **20 minutes**
Cooking **25 minutes**

Matthew's SPICED CHOCOLATE FUDGE CAKES WITH CREME ANGLAISE

The red and blue teams were challenged to prepare a business class meal for serving on a Qantas A380. For Gary, Matthew's fudge cakes were "the dish of the day, or even the month". Matthew added a little Chinese five-spice to flavour these almost-fondant fudge cakes, making them a great dessert to serve after any meal with an Asian theme.

250g unsalted butter, chopped, plus extra, softened, to grease
25g (¼ cup) Dutch cocoa*
250g dark chocolate (70% cocoa solids), chopped
110g (½ cup) caster sugar
5 eggs
5 egg yolks

120g plain flour
2 tsp Chinese five-spice
105g (¾ cup) macadamias, roughly chopped
GINGER CREME ANGLAISE
410ml (1²⁄₃ cups) pouring cream
80ml (⅓ cup) milk

1 vanilla bean, split, seeds scraped
6 egg yolks
110g (½ cup) caster sugar
5cm piece ginger, finely grated

1 To make crème anglaise, combine cream, milk, vanilla bean and seeds in a saucepan and bring almost to the boil. Place egg yolks and sugar in a bowl and whisk until thick and pale. Whisking continuously, gradually add milk mixture to egg yolk mixture, then return mixture to the pan over low heat. Add ginger and, using a wooden spoon, stir continuously until thick enough to coat the back of the spoon (don't boil the mixture). Strain through a fine sieve into a large bowl, then whisk gently for 2 minutes to reduce heat. Cool.

2 Preheat oven to 200°C. Grease eight 160ml (²⁄₃-cup) dariole moulds with extra softened butter. Place cocoa in a fine sieve and dust bases and sides of the moulds, shaking out excess cocoa.

3 Place butter and chocolate in a heatproof bowl over a saucepan of gently simmering water and stir occasionally until melted and smooth. Set aside to cool for 10 minutes.

4 Using an electric mixer, whisk sugar, eggs and yolks until thick and pale. Add chocolate mixture and, using a metal spoon, fold in until combined. Sift flour with five-spice into chocolate mixture, add 70g (½ cup) macadamias and gently fold in until just combined. Divide batter among moulds and place on an oven tray. Bake for 12 minutes or until firm (the longer you leave cakes in the oven, the less runny the centres will be). Remove from oven and cool for 15 minutes in the moulds (they will collapse if removed too soon).

5 Run a knife around the inside of the moulds, then turn out cakes onto plates. Drizzle with crème anglaise and scatter with macadamias.

DUTCH COCOA has a more concentrated flavour and deeper colour than regular cocoa and is available from delis.

George Calombaris

George Calombaris has been awarded more accolades for his work than most receive in a lifetime, and this exuberant chef is still only 31. Before joining the MasterChef team for Series 1, George had been voted one of the Top 40 Chefs of Influence in the World by *Global Food and Wine Magazine*. An internationally successful restaurateur, George owns three restaurants in Melbourne and one in Mykonos, Greece. His flagship Melbourne restaurant, The Press Club, was awarded *The Age Good Food Guide* Best New Restaurant 2008, with George named Chef of the Year 2008. In the same year *The Age Melbourne Magazine* placed George in its Top 100 Most Influential People list.

George uses firm and direct guidance to push the MasterChef contestants to improve and strive for excellence in their cooking. The losing blue team from the Qantas challenge faced his **carrot cake with cream cheese icing** for their elimination challenge. They were to name every ingredient.

After being star of his team in the Qantas challenge, Matthew came undone with the carrot cake. "I was disappointed after I said dried apricots instead of jam, because I knew 13 of the 16 ingredients in this cake."

Serves **12**
Preparation **30 minutes**
Cooking **1 hour 5 minutes**

CARROT CAKE WITH CREAM CHEESE ICING

150ml extra virgin olive oil
150ml grape seed oil
1 tsp vanilla extract
4 eggs
330g (1½ cups firmly packed) dark brown sugar
3 carrots, peeled, coarsely grated
100g sultanas
75g (¾ cup) walnuts, finely chopped

50g pecans, finely chopped
50g pistachios, halved, plus extra, chopped, to serve
300g (2 cups) plain flour
2 tsp baking powder
1 tsp bicarbonate of soda
2 tsp ground cinnamon, plus extra, to dust
¾ tsp ground cumin
½ tsp ground cloves

110g (⅓ cup) apricot jam
CREAM CHEESE ICING
185g unsalted butter, softened
185g cream cheese, chopped, softened
375g icing sugar, sifted
2 lemons, zested, plus 1 tsp juice

1 Preheat oven to 180°C. Grease a deep 23cm round cake pan, then line the base and side with baking paper.* Mix together olive oil, grape seed oil and vanilla extract in a jug.

2 Using an electric mixer, beat eggs and sugar on high speed for 5 minutes or until thick and pale. Reduce speed to low and, with the motor running, add the oil mixture in a thin, steady stream until well combined and emulsified.

3 Add carrots, sultanas, walnuts, pecans and pistachios to the bowl, but don't fold in yet. Sift flour, baking powder, bicarbonate of soda, ½ tsp salt and spices over the top. Using a large spoon, fold in until just combined.

4 Spoon batter into cake pan, then bake on the bottom shelf of the oven for 45 minutes. Cover with baking paper to prevent overbrowning and bake for a further 20 minutes or until a skewer inserted into the centre of the cake comes out clean. Transfer to a wire rack, cool completely in the pan, then turn out onto a plate.

5 **To make cream cheese icing,** using an electric mixer, beat butter on high speed until pale and fluffy. Add cream cheese, piece by piece, and beat until pale and fluffy. Reduce speed to low, then gradually beat in icing sugar until just combined. Add lemon zest and juice and stir to combine.

6 **To make apricot glaze,** place jam and ½ tbs water in a small pan over low heat and simmer, stirring, for 4 minutes or until syrupy. Using a pastry brush, brush the glaze over the top and side of the cake. Cool for 5 minutes.

7 Using a spatula, spread the icing in a smooth layer over the top of the cake, then, using the tip of the spatula or the back of a spoon, create ripples in the icing. Scatter with extra pistachios and dust with cinnamon to serve.

TO LINE A ROUND CAKE PAN trace around the base of the pan onto a sheet of baking paper, then cut out the round. To determine the length of paper required to line the side, pull paper from roll and wrap around the outside of the pan. Tear off paper and place lengthwise on a work surface. Fold over the paper towards you, then repeat, leaving a 1.5cm-wide border along the long edge. Using scissors, cut the border at 1cm intervals to fray the edge **(PIC 1)**. Grease the pan, then line the side with paper, slit-edge down. The slits should sit flat over the base, while the folded part forms a collar extending 3–4cm above the rim of the pan **(PIC 2)**. To line the base of the pan, place the round over the slits **(PIC 3)**. Your pan is now ready to use. **EXTENDING THE PAPER** above the rim of the pan acts as a shield against heat, preventing the cake top from overbrowning.

Chapter Five

PARIS OR BUST

The Top 8 fly to London and feast with Heston Blumenthal.
"Le super-challenge" sees teams racing across Paris, while, back in the
kitchen, three old friends hatch plans for a second chance. Margaret Fulton
high-fives her way into an invention test, an army marches on its
stomach, and macarons create a "world of pain". Greed serves Alvin well.

Makes **20**
Preparation **1 hour**
+ **1 hour 15 minutes** refrigeration
Cooking **35 minutes**

Callum's VIOLET MACARONS WITH RASPBERRY MOUSSE & BERRIES

The Crown Jewels were brought out for the first London challenge. Each contestant had three hours to produce an Imperial Crown-inspired pastry, fit to sit on the cake plate at The Langham Hotel's afternoon tea. Callum's violet macarons won him a private masterclass with Jamie Oliver. He chose Jono to go with him, and got the biggest hug of the series.

220g raspberries (you need 72)
180g blueberries (you need 24)
MACARONS
220g (1⅓ cups) icing sugar
120g (1 cup) ground almonds
3 egg whites
55g (¼ cup) caster sugar
½ tsp violet essence, to taste

2–3 drops purple food
  colouring
ITALIAN MERINGUE
55g (¼ cup) caster sugar
1 tsp liquid glucose
1 egg white
RASPBERRY MOUSSE
375g raspberries, puréed, sieved

2 x 5g leaves titanium-strength
  gelatine
50ml cream, whipped to soft
  peaks
BUTTER ICING
100g butter, softened
120g (¾ cup) icing sugar, sifted

1 To make macarons, preheat oven to 120°C. Grease 2 large oven trays and line with baking paper. Sift icing sugar and ground almonds together 3 times. Using an electric mixer, whisk egg whites until stiff peaks form, then gradually add sugar and whisk until thick and glossy. Add violet essence and food colouring and whisk to combine. Fold in almond mixture.

2 Transfer to a piping bag fitted with a plain 2cm nozzle. Pipe 4cm rounds onto the trays. Gently tap the trays underneath to level the mixture and remove any air pockets. Leave to stand, uncovered, for 20 minutes so macarons form a skin.

3 Bake for 30 minutes or until macarons can be lifted off the tray. Cool on the trays for 10 minutes, then carefully transfer to a wire rack for 30 minutes to cool completely.

4 To make Italian meringue, combine sugar, glucose and 2 tbs of water in a small saucepan. Stir over low heat without boiling until sugar has dissolved, then increase heat to medium–high and bring to the boil. Cook for 5 minutes (or until 121°C on a sugar thermometer). Using an electric mixer, whisk egg white to soft peaks. With mixer running at high speed, slowly add hot syrup in a thin stream down the side of the bowl. Continue whisking for 8–10 minutes or until mixture is cold. Set aside.

5 To make raspberry mousse, heat 50ml of the purée in a small saucepan until warm. Soak gelatine leaves in a small bowl of cold water for 5 minutes. Squeeze out excess water and stir into warm purée until dissolved. Stir into remaining purée in a large bowl. Fold in the cream and Italian meringue. Refrigerate for 1 hour or until set.

6 To make butter icing, use an electric mixer to beat butter and icing sugar for 5 minutes or until light and fluffy. Spoon into a piping bag fitted with a 1cm star nozzle.

7 To assemble the macarons, pipe 4 rosettes of icing onto the flat side of a macaron. Place 3 raspberries between the icing rosettes, then top with a tablespoon of mousse. Sandwich with another macaron, then dab a little butter icing on top and place a blueberry on the icing.

"That looks spectacular. That's the plate I'd go for." Gary

Serves **4**
Preparation **25 minutes**
Cooking **55 minutes**

Marion's BALLOTINE OF TRUFFLED CHICKEN

"Le super-challenge" was a race from London to Paris, ending in the most beautiful kitchen in the world on the banks of the River Seine. After almost missing the train from London with ticket problems, Marion and Callum just couldn't find the truffle shop. But, despite their time pressures, they couldn't resist pausing under the Eiffel Tower to admire the view.

4 chicken marylands
200g foie gras
200g butter, softened
2 tsp chopped truffle

4 slices truffle
450g mixed mushrooms,
    including morels
60ml (¼ cup) truffled brandy*

2 tbs double cream
Chervil sprigs, to serve

1 Remove the skin from each chicken maryland in one piece. Cut the thigh meat from the bone and flatten out slightly (you won't need the drumsticks for this recipe, so cook separately for another meal). Combine the foie gras, 100g of the butter, the chopped truffle and a pinch of salt. Spread over the underside of the thigh meat and roll up to enclose.

2 Stuff a rolled thigh into each drumstick pocket of the chicken skin and cut off the excess skin, allowing for a little shrinkage during cooking. Place a truffle slice between the skin and thigh, on the presentation side. Wrap very tightly in plastic wrap to form a neat sausage shape. Poach the chicken in a pan of barely simmering water for 40 minutes.

3 Meanwhile, melt 50g of the remaining butter in a large frying pan over medium–high heat. Add the mushrooms and cook, stirring occasionally, for 8 minutes or until soft and lightly golden. Deglaze with the truffled brandy, then stir in the cream.

4 Remove the chicken from the water and unwrap. Melt the remaining butter in a frying pan and cook the ballotines over medium–high heat, turning frequently, for 5 minutes or until browned. Slice and serve with the mushrooms and chervil sprigs.

IN PLACE OF TRUFFLED BRANDY, infuse ½ tsp chopped truffle in 60ml (¼ cup) brandy for 2 hours, then strain.

Marion won the Heston Blumenthal challenge in the UK and went into another celebrity chef challenge. "Marion doesn't need an immunity pin. She loves this. She's smiling all the time," said chef Martin Blunos.

Callum's CHOCOLATE CROISSANT PUDDINGS

For Callum, the race to Paris was "the most enjoyable challenge I've ever done". The day was hard, but rewarding, especially for Callum, who'd been planning a chocolate fondant dessert but couldn't find couverture chocolate in the French market. He put on "le thinking cap" and came up with this Gallic version of the English favourite, bread and butter pudding.

50g (⅓ cup) raisins
60ml (¼ cup) brandy
300ml pouring cream
6 egg yolks
55g (¼ cup) caster sugar

2 chocolate croissants,* torn into
 2cm pieces
40g dark chocolate
 (70% cocoa solids), roughly
 chopped

Roasted hazelnuts, strawberries,
 pomegranate seeds and
 mascarpone, to serve

1 Preheat oven to 160°C. Lightly grease four 180ml (¾-cup) dariole moulds. Cut four 3 x 24cm strips of baking paper and place a strip in each mould to partially line the base and side and extend above the rim (this helps remove the puddings from the moulds).
2 Combine raisins and brandy in a bowl and leave to soak until needed.
3 Place cream in a saucepan and bring to a simmer over medium heat. Whisk egg yolks and sugar in a bowl until thick and pale. Gradually add cream, whisking continuously until well combined. Add torn croissants and soak for 10 minutes.
4 Fill each mould halfway with croissant mixture, then top with one-quarter of the chocolate and then the remaining croissant mixture. Bake puddings for 25 minutes or until custard is set. Cool for 5 minutes, then lift out onto plates.
5 To serve, spoon brandied raisins over puddings and scatter with hazelnuts, strawberries and pomegranate seeds. Serve with mascarpone.

CHOCOLATE CROISSANTS are widely available from supermarkets and bakeries.

"Have your French inspirations made it onto the plate? If there's a place to show off your skills, then this is it."

"I want to get up and dance because this dessert is so beautiful!" George

Courtney's GRILLED PRAWNS WITH FENNEL, ORANGE & APPLE SALAD

When the Top 7 returned from London they were invited to a "learn to taste and critique" lunch with Matt Preston. They were served six dishes and gave their frank opinions. Then a familiar curry appeared and there were murmurings of realisation... some old friends had returned to the kitchen. Those who cooked the three best dishes of the day – Courtney, Peter and Jimmy – made it back for a second chance and the Top 7 became the Top 10 again.

16 medium green prawns, peeled,
    deveined, tails intact
1 lemon, zested
1/2 tsp finely diced red chilli
2 tbs olive oil
VINAIGRETTE
1 tbs Dijon mustard

80ml (1/3 cup) olive oil
2 tbs honey
1 tbs red wine vinegar
2 tbs lemon juice
1/2 lemon, zested
SALAD
1 celery heart,* finely sliced

2 baby fennel bulbs, very finely
    sliced,* fronds reserved
2 oranges, segmented
2 granny smith apples, cut into
    julienne (matchsticks)
1 cup roughly chopped parsley

1 Place prawns in a large bowl with lemon zest, chilli and olive oil. Marinate in the fridge for 15 minutes.
2 To make vinaigrette, whisk together all the ingredients and set aside.
3 To make the salad, toss all the ingredients in a large bowl.
4 Preheat a barbecue grill plate or large chargrill pan over high heat. Cook the prawns for 2 minutes on each side or until they change colour and are cooked through. Toss the salad with half of the dressing and spoon onto serving plates. Top with the prawns, drizzle with the remaining dressing and scatter with fennel fronds.

IF YOU HAVE A MANDOLIN, use it to slice the celery and fennel. It will give beautiful paper-thin slices.

Good food doesn't have to be complicated. This simple dish was good enough for Courtney to win back her white apron.

Peter's **PAN-FRIED DORY ON SMASHED POTATOES WITH PRAWN BISQUE**

This was Peter's answer to the second-chance challenge. "When presented with a beautiful fresh John Dory, I just had to cook it. I needed to dig deep and cook something special to get back in. With its big, bold flavours, this is one of my proudest culinary achievements."

4 John Dory fillets
1 tbs olive oil
80g butter
Micro herbs and extra virgin olive oil, to serve
PRAWN BISQUE
60ml (¼ cup) olive oil
1 leek, white part only, diced

1 fennel bulb, finely diced
2 carrots, finely diced
2 cloves garlic, finely diced
Heads and shells of 12 large prawns
1 tbs tomato paste
250ml (1 cup) white wine*
500ml (2 cups) fish stock

4 stalks parsley, chopped
125ml (½ cup) pouring cream
SMASHED POTATOES
3 large sebago potatoes (800g), scrubbed
75g butter
¼ cup finely chopped flat-leaf parsley

1 To make prawn bisque, heat the oil in a large saucepan. Add the leek, fennel, carrots and garlic and cook over low–medium heat for 10 minutes or until softened. Increase the heat and add the prawn shells and heads. Cook, stirring occasionally, for 5 minutes or until caramelised. Add the tomato paste and cook for a further 2 minutes. Deglaze the pan with white wine, then add stock and parsley, and season well. Bring to the boil, reduce the heat to very low and simmer for 20 minutes.

2 Cool the bisque slightly and process in 2 batches in a food processor until smooth. Pass the bisque through a fine sieve and return to a clean saucepan. Bring to a slow simmer, add cream and stir to combine. Adjust seasoning if required.

3 Meanwhile, to make smashed potatoes, place unpeeled potatoes into a saucepan of salted water. Bring to the boil and cook the potatoes for 10 minutes or until soft when tested with a skewer. Drain potatoes and allow to cool slightly.

4 Peel the skins from potatoes and roughly chop into small even-sized pieces. Heat the butter in a frying pan and add potatoes. Season well with salt and freshly ground black pepper. Fry until crisp. Remove potatoes from heat and add parsley.

5 Diagonally score the skin on the fish fillets 3–4 times and season generously with salt. Heat half the oil in a large frying pan. Cook the fish, skin-side down, in 2 batches for 2 minutes or until skin is golden and crisp. Gently flip fish and add half the butter to the pan. Fry for a further minute. Set aside and cover loosely with foil to keep warm.

6 To serve, place a 9cm metal ring mould in the middle of each large soup plate. Press one-quarter of the potatoes into the ring, then lift off to form a potato stack. Place a fish fillet, skin-side up, on top of the potato stack. Top with micro herbs. Pour prawn bisque around to reach halfway up the potato stack. Drizzle the fish with extra virgin olive oil to serve.

REPLACE THE WHITE WINE with 60ml (¼ cup) ouzo for a beautiful, unique anise flavour.

Jonathan's WHITE CHOCOLATE POTS WITH RHUBARB COMPOTE

Snails were in the mystery box this week, but not everyone used them. Jonathan pulled another French classic out of his hat to win the best dish. "I had to force myself not to use the snails in this challenge. But I was so excited to cook another dish based on the French classic pot au crème, served simply with a few crisp snap biscuits."

300g white chocolate, roughly chopped
300ml pouring cream
2 cinnamon quills
4 egg yolks
110g (½ cup) caster sugar

4 stalks rhubarb, trimmed, cut into 2cm pieces
1 tbs white balsamic vinegar
PISTACHIO SNAPS
75g unsalted butter, softened
110g (½ cup) caster sugar

2 egg whites
70g (½ cup) pistachios, finely ground
35g (¼ cup) plain flour
Icing sugar, to dust

1 To make pots, place chocolate in a large heatproof bowl over a saucepan of gently simmering water and stir until melted (don't let bowl touch the water).

2 Meanwhile, place cream and cinnamon in a small saucepan and bring almost to the boil. Place egg yolks and 55g (¼ cup) sugar in a bowl and whisk until thick and pale. Whisking continuously, gradually add cream mixture to egg yolk mixture, then return to pan over low heat and, using a wooden spoon, stir continuously (do not boil) until thick enough to coat the back of the spoon. Strain through a fine sieve into melted chocolate and stir well. Place chocolate mixture over a bowl of iced water to cool, then spoon into six 180ml (¾-cup) glasses and refrigerate overnight.

3 To make rhubarb compote, place rhubarb, remaining 55g (¼ cup) sugar, 180ml (¾ cup) water and vinegar in a small saucepan over medium heat. Cook, stirring occasionally, for 15 minutes or until rhubarb is just tender. Set aside to cool completely.

4 To make pistachio snaps, preheat oven to 160°C. Using an electric mixer, beat butter and sugar until pale and fluffy. Add egg whites and beat until well combined. Stir in pistachios, flour and a pinch of salt. Spoon mixture into a piping bag fitted with a 5mm plain nozzle and pipe thin, 3cm-long lines, 5cm apart, onto 2 oven trays lined with baking paper. Bake for 10 minutes or until edges are light golden. Remove from oven and immediately twist snaps. (If snaps cool, you won't be able to twist them. To re-warm, return to oven.) Return snaps to trays and cool.

5 Spoon rhubarb compote over white chocolate pots. Dust pistachio snaps with icing sugar and serve with pots.

After this great start, Jonathan's week went downhill. In the Country Women's Association baking challenge his fruitcakes were uncooked inside. The feisty CWA ladies were not amused.

Serves **4**
Preparation **45 minutes**
Cooking **1 hour 20 minutes**

Claire's FRIED MASTERSTOCK CHICKEN WITH CHILLI CARAMEL & ORANGE SALT

The home-style invention test came with a big dose of inspiration in the shape of the irrepressible Margaret Fulton, queen of Australian home-cooking. She bustled in, high-fived the judges and set the standard high. Gary just loved this dish: "Bloody beautiful! Soft succulent chicken with crispy skin; sweet, but with a hint of chilli." Claire's talents came to the fore in the final weeks of competition. She loved baking fruitcake for the ladies of the CWA and cooked against two celebrity chefs, Adam Melonas and Shaun Presland.

1 x 1.6kg chicken
Vegetable oil, to deep–fry
MASTERSTOCK*
375ml (1½ cups) light soy sauce
375ml (1½ cups) cooking sake*
1 tsp ground star anise
1½ cinnamon quills

5cm piece ginger,
  finely chopped
4 cloves garlic, chopped
440g (2 cups) sugar
3 long strips orange
  peel

CHILLI CARAMEL
220g (1 cup) sugar
2 tsp dried chilli flakes
250ml (1 cup) masterstock
ORANGE SALT
½ orange, zested
1 tbs rock salt

1 To make masterstock, combine all the ingredients in a large stockpot with 5L water and bring to the boil over high heat. Reduce heat to medium and simmer for 20 minutes.

2 To make chilli caramel, place sugar in a small saucepan and add 250ml (1 cup) water. Stir over low–medium heat without boiling until sugar has dissolved. Brush down the side of the pan with a pastry brush dipped in water to dissolve any crystals. Increase heat to medium–high and cook, without stirring, for 15 minutes or until a light caramel colour. Add the chilli flakes and carefully (it will spit) stir in the 250ml (1 cup) masterstock. The toffee will harden, so stir until dissolved into the stock.

3 Bring 2L water to the boil in a large saucepan. Add the chicken and blanch for 5 minutes. Remove from the pan. Place chicken into remaining masterstock. Simmer, covered, for 20 minutes, then turn chicken and simmer for a further 5 minutes. Turn off heat and leave, covered, for 15 minutes.

4 Remove chicken from masterstock, cool slightly and cut in half. Pat dry with paper towel. Fill a large wok or saucepan one-third full with oil and heat over medium heat to 180°C (or until a cube of bread turns golden in 10 seconds). Deep-fry half the chicken for 6 minutes, turning halfway, until dark golden. Drain on paper towel. Repeat with remaining chicken half. Cut up the chicken Chinese-style and drizzle with half the chilli caramel.

5 To make orange salt, pound orange zest and salt together using a mortar and pestle. Serve chicken with remaining chilli caramel and orange salt.

MASTERSTOCK is a Chinese-style spiced stock, used for poaching. It is traditionally re-used many times, allowing rich flavours to develop. Care must be taken to avoid spoilage. We recommend keeping for up to 1 week in the fridge or freezing for up to 1 month. Bring to the boil before using. Claire's method of poaching the chicken in masterstock infuses it with flavour before frying. **COOKING SAKE** is available from Asian grocers and some large supermarkets.

"They say you can never trust a thin cook. But you can obviously trust Claire." Margaret Fulton

Makes **40**
Preparation **40 minutes**
+ **30 minutes refrigeration**
Cooking **1 hour 10 minutes**

Adam's GREEN TEA DUMPLINGS WITH CHICKEN

Matt Preston loved the way these simple dumplings were spiked with chilli oil and flavoured vinegar. For Adam, this is true home-style cooking: "I'll often spend a few hours filling the freezer with dumplings. That way a great meal is never more than a few minutes away."

500ml (2 cups) masterstock*
60ml (1/4 cup) peanut oil
CHILLI OIL
125ml (1/2 cup) peanut oil
2 tbs chopped onion
3 cloves garlic, chopped
2 tbs dried chilli flakes
DUMPLING DOUGH
2 tbs green tea leaves

300g (2 cups) plain flour
FILLING
4 chicken thigh fillets (about 550g), chopped
1/2 small onion, chopped
3 cloves garlic, chopped
4cm piece ginger, finely chopped
1 tsp salt

2 tsp soy sauce
1 tsp sake
1/3 cup chopped coriander
2 tbs chopped chives
ORANGE & GINGER VINEGAR
1 orange, juiced
4cm piece ginger, cut into julienne (matchsticks)
60ml (1/4 cup) rice wine vinegar

1 Preheat oven to 65°C. To make chilli oil, place the oil in a small ovenproof saucepan and heat over medium heat. Add onion and garlic and cook for 2 minutes or until soft and just starting to colour. Turn off heat, add chilli and season with salt. Cook in the oven for 1 hour. Strain, discarding the solids.

2 To make dumpling dough, combine tea leaves with 375ml (1½ cups) water in a small saucepan and bring to the boil. Turn off heat and leave for 1 minute, then strain. Sift flour into a bowl and make a well in the centre. Bring tea back to the boil and pour 250ml (1 cup) onto the flour. Add a pinch of salt and stir with a wooden spoon, then your hands, until dough comes together. Turn out onto a floured surface and knead for 5 minutes or until silky. Wrap in plastic wrap and rest for 30 minutes.

3 For filling, combine all ingredients, except herbs, in a food processor. Process in short bursts to form a rough paste. Season well and stir in herbs. Refrigerate for 30 minutes for flavours to develop.

4 For orange and ginger vinegar, place orange juice in a small saucepan and bring just to the boil. Reduce heat to medium and simmer for 2 minutes or until reduced by half. Stir in the ginger and vinegar and remove from the heat.

5 To assemble the dumplings, divide dough in half. Roll each portion into a log about 20cm long, and cut into 20 pieces. Roll out each piece to make 10cm rounds, 1mm-thick. Place 3 tsp of filling in the centre of each, fold up the edges and pleat to seal well.

6 Heat half the oil in a large frying pan and cook half the dumplings over medium–high heat for 2 minutes or until bases are browned. Pour hot water into pan to come two-thirds up the sides of the dumplings. Cover pan and cook for 2 minutes, then uncover and cook until all liquid has evaporated and dumplings begin to fry again. Repeat with remaining dumplings.

7 Serve dumplings with chilli oil, orange and ginger vinegar, and masterstock.

USE MASTERSTOCK from previous recipe (page 202) to serve with this dish. The two dishes are ideal as a meal.

Adriano Zumbo

The Torte Torturer, the Patissier of Pain, Balmain's King of Cakes... whatever you like to call him, Adriano Zumbo has become a figure of terror and trepidation in the MasterChef kitchen. The pressure-test croquembouche of Series 1 still haunts the dreams of former contestants. What would renowned pastry chef Adriano devise for Series 2? A **macaron tower** of 120 perfect, flavoured, coloured macarons, of course!

The judges would be inspecting the look, the clarity of flavours and the quality of the macarons and their fillings. Macarons should be crunchy on the outside with a classic crisp dome, and soft and chewy when you bite into them. This tower is made of red macarons with raspberry and beetroot filling, and purple macarons filled with olive ganache. These may sound savoury, but the result is sweet.

The contestants spend four hours "in a world of pain". Peter's tower is the least impressive, sending him home for the second time. "Now I can't look at oysters, or macarons," he groaned afterwards.

Serves **30–50**
Preparation **3 hours**
Cooking **3 hours 10 minutes**

1

THE MACARON TOWER

900g caster sugar
1½ tbs red food colouring*
660g egg whites
2 tsp powdered egg whites*
900g ground almonds
900g icing sugar
2 tsp black food colouring*
1 tbs maroon or burgundy food
  colouring*

RASPBERRY JAM
500g frozen raspberries
50g packet Jam Setta (pectin)*
165g caster sugar
BEETROOT BUTTERCREAM
220g caster sugar
150g whole eggs
90g egg yolks
400g unsalted butter, cut into
  1cm cubes, softened
9g (3 tsp) beetroot powder*

KALAMATA OLIVE GANACHE
300g pitted kalamata olives
220g caster sugar
1½ tsp vanilla bean paste
500g white chocolate, chopped
80g unsalted butter, cut into 1cm
  cubes, softened
80ml (⅓ cup) extra virgin
  olive oil

1 To make red macarons, place 450g caster sugar and 125ml (½ cup) water in a small saucepan over low heat and stir until sugar dissolves. Brush down the side of the pan with a wet pastry brush to prevent sugar crystals forming. Increase heat to low–medium, bring to the boil, then stir in red colouring. Cook until syrup reaches 121°C on a sugar thermometer **(PIC 1)**.

• Mix 165g egg whites and 1 tsp powdered egg whites in an electric mixer until just combined. As soon as syrup reaches 121°C, with the mixer running on medium speed, pour hot syrup in a thin, steady stream down the side of the bowl. Whisk for 5 minutes or until thick and glossy, then whisk for a further 3 minutes until cooled completely.

• Sift 450g each ground almonds and icing sugar into a large bowl. Pour in 165g egg whites, but don't stir yet. Stir in one-quarter of the meringue, then stir in remaining meringue. Spoon into 2 large piping bags fitted with 1.5cm plain nozzles **(PIC 2)**. Pipe 4cm rounds, 2cm apart, onto 6 large oven trays lined with baking paper (mixture makes 150 rounds). Bang trays gently on a work surface to flatten any peaks in the macarons. If any remain, dip a finger in water and press gently to flatten. Leave for 30 minutes for a skin to form on the macarons. To test if ready, touch the top quickly; you should be able to remove your finger without leaving a mark.

2 To make raspberry jam, place all ingredients in small saucepan over medium heat and stir until sugar dissolves. Simmer for 10 minutes or until thickened. (Dip a chilled spoon into mixture, then remove and run your finger along back of spoon; line should remain.) Push jam through a fine sieve into a bowl, discarding seeds. Cover surface of jam with plastic wrap and refrigerate for 30 minutes to set.

3 To make beetroot buttercream, place 80ml (⅓ cup) water and sugar in a small saucepan over low heat and stir until sugar dissolves. Brush down side of the pan with a wet pastry brush to prevent sugar crystals forming. Increase heat to low–medium and boil until syrup reaches 118°C on a sugar thermometer. Using an electric mixer, whisk eggs and egg yolks until just combined.

Of course, if you don't want to make a tower, you can simply bake and fill the macarons. They will keep in a tin in the fridge for 5 days.

- With the mixer running on medium speed, pour hot syrup in a thin, steady stream down the side of the bowl and whisk for 3 minutes or until mixture cools to 50°C. Add butter, piece by piece, whisking until combined after each addition. Add beetroot powder and beat until well combined.
- Transfer buttercream to a piping bag fitted with a 1cm plain nozzle. Refrigerate to firm slightly.

4 To bake red macarons, preheat oven to 200°C. Place 3 trays of macarons in oven, then turn off oven and leave for 10 minutes. Turn oven back on to 155°C and bake, swapping trays halfway, for a further 10 minutes, or until macarons can be removed easily from trays. (Lower tray may need longer.)
- Remove macarons from oven and leave on trays for 10 minutes to cool. Meanwhile, increase oven to 200°C and bake remaining 3 trays of red macarons. Cool completely.

5 To fill red macarons, whisk raspberry jam until smooth and put in piping bag with a 1cm plain nozzle. Pipe a round of the buttercream onto half the red macarons, leaving a 1cm border, then pipe jam into centre of buttercream **(PIC 3)**. Sandwich with remaining red macarons. Put on trays and refrigerate.

6 To make purple macarons, repeat step 1, using black and maroon colouring. To bake, repeat step 4.

7 To make kalamata olive ganache, place 250g olives in a small pan and cover with water. Bring to the boil, then drain. Repeat 5 times to remove saltiness. Return olives to pan with sugar, 125ml (½ cup) water and vanilla. Cook over medium heat for 40 minutes to candy. Drain, discarding syrup. Process candied olives in a food processor to a paste. Rinse remaining 50g olives and finely chop.
- Place chocolate in a heatproof bowl over a pan of gently simmering water and stir until melted (don't let the bowl touch the water). Stir in olive paste. Whisk in butter, piece by piece, until well combined after each addition. Whisking continuously, gradually pour oil in a thin, steady stream and whisk until emulsified. Stir in chopped olives, then refrigerate olive ganache to cool slightly.
- Spoon into a piping bag fitted with a 1cm plain nozzle. Pipe ganache onto half the purple macarons, leaving a 5mm border. Sandwich with the remaining purple macarons.

8 To assemble macaron tower, insert wooden toothpicks, tilted upwards, into a polystyrene cone 3cm apart. Starting at the bottom of the cone and alternating between red and purple macarons, push a macaron onto each toothpick, without going all the way through. Reserve smaller macarons for top.

PROFESSIONAL GRADE concentrated colouring and **POWDERED EGG WHITES** are from cake decorating shops. **JAM SETTA** is from the baking section of supermarkets. **BEETROOT POWDER** is available from Herbie's Spices in Sydney or by mail order (herbies.com.au).

Serves **6**
Preparation **30 minutes**
Cooking **1 hour 5 minutes**

Courtney's MEATBALLS WITH TOMATO SAUCE

The army challenge was Courtney's favourite team task. "When we were marching to the outdoor kitchen we had no idea what equipment or ingredients would be there. But we did have a plan: 'Give the men meat!' The 100 soldiers hadn't had a hot meal in more than three weeks so our plan was for hearty comfort food. The tomato sauce was the first dish to go on: there were plenty of herbs so it was easy to get lots of flavour into it. Tray after tray of meatballs went into that sauce, but that pile of mince just didn't seem to get any smaller!"

Grated parmesan, to serve
HERB & TOMATO SAUCE
60ml (¼ cup) olive oil
1 large onion, finely chopped
2 cloves garlic, crushed
1 tsp sea salt
1 large carrot, diced
6 thyme sprigs
2 tbs tomato paste

2 x 400g cans diced tomatoes
1 tsp dried Italian herbs
1 tsp dried oregano
1 tbs sugar
1 cup fresh basil leaves
MEATBALLS
700g beef mince
1 tsp sea salt
1 tsp finely chopped rosemary

1 tsp dried Italian herbs
½ tsp chicken stock powder
1 egg
25g (¼ cup) packaged
    breadcrumbs
1 tbs tomato paste
1 tsp mild paprika
2 tbs tomato ketchup
1 tsp thyme leaves

1 To make the sauce, heat the oil in a large saucepan over medium heat. Add the onion, garlic and salt, and cook for 5 minutes or until beginning to soften. Add the carrot and thyme sprigs and cook for a further 2 minutes or until soft. Stir in the remaining ingredients, except the basil. Bring to the boil, then reduce the heat to low, cover the pan and simmer gently for 45 minutes or until thickened.

2 Meanwhile, to make the meatballs, combine all the ingredients and season with ground black pepper. Use your hands to mix well. Roll into balls, using 2 tbs mixture for each.

3 Add meatballs to simmering sauce without stirring, increase heat to medium and cook for 15 minutes, or until cooked through. Gently stir in basil leaves and top with parmesan. Serve with pasta or bread.

Courtney's meatballs were the army challenge's dish of the day. "They're great – sweet and rich. And look, that bloke over there is licking his plate."

"That's fabulous! The hundred lads that come in and taste these aren't going to want to march back out again." George

Jonathan's RHUBARB & APPLE CRUMBLE WITH CUSTARD

The army challenge was a highlight for many contestants, especially when they produced such great food that the judges gave them a standing ovation. Jonathan thoroughly enjoyed cooking up the blue team's desserts. "We all worked so hard as a team under Adam's great leadership. The crumble is an old favourite of mine – I love crumble! This was similar to my childhood memory dish from that very first day in the MasterChef kitchen."

2 bunches rhubarb, trimmed,
  cut into 2cm pieces
1 lemon, juiced
110g (1/2 cup) caster sugar
40g (1/4 cup) sultanas
2 x 400g cans pie apple

CRUMBLE
225g (1¹/₂ cups) plain flour
110g (1/2 cup firmly packed)
  brown sugar
45g (1/2 cup) desiccated coconut
150g unsalted butter, chopped

CUSTARD
375ml (1¹/₂ cups) milk
125ml (1/2 cup) pouring cream
4 egg yolks
1/3 cup (75 g) caster sugar
1 tbs cornflour
1 tsp vanilla extract

1 Preheat the oven to 180°C. Put rhubarb, lemon juice and sugar in a large saucepan. Cover and cook, stirring occasionally, over low–medium heat for 8 minutes or until the rhubarb is tender. Add the sultanas and pie apple and stir to combine. Transfer to a 1.5L (6-cup) ovenproof dish.

2 To make crumble, combine the flour, sugar and coconut in a bowl. Use your fingertips to rub in the butter, until the mixture resembles coarse breadcrumbs. Spread over the fruit mixture. Bake for 35 minutes until golden.

3 To make custard, heat milk and cream in a saucepan until almost at boiling point. Meanwhile, use a wire whisk to beat yolks, sugar and cornflour in a bowl until creamy. Pour the hot milk mixture onto the egg mixture, whisking continuously. Pour into a clean saucepan and stir over low heat for 5 minutes or until the custard has thickened enough to coat the back of a spoon (do not allow to boil). Stir in the vanilla extract and serve with the crumble.

Adam had to make some strategic decisions as he chose his team for the army challenge. "My first pick is Marion, because that's the rules!"

Claire's PRAWN & FENNEL SALAD WITH PRAWN OIL

Gary tasted Claire's prawn-and-pandan mystery box dish and was blown away. "This is a lovely, clean, sophisticated little dish. The fennel purée is delicious – smooth and slightly aniseed." Claire blowtorched the prawns for presentation and it gave them "a little waft of chargrill – they're like something you'd find in a sushi bar. Just delicious".

250ml (1 cup) olive oil
12 medium green king prawns, peeled, deveined, tails left intact, heads and shells reserved

5 bulbs baby fennel, trimmed, fronds reserved
300ml pouring cream
2 tbs white wine vinegar
Sliced grilled baguette, to serve

1 To make the prawn oil,* heat 125ml (½ cup) of the oil in a large saucepan over high heat. Add the prawn heads and shells and cook, stirring, for 6 minutes or until shells are crisp and turn pink. Remove from heat and leave for 20 minutes for flavours to infuse oil. Season with salt.

2 Meanwhile, to make fennel purée, finely chop 3 of the fennel bulbs. Combine with the cream in a saucepan and gently bring to the boil over low–medium heat. Simmer for 20 minutes or until fennel can be crushed with the back of a spoon. Drain, reserving 60ml (¼ cup) cream. Purée the fennel and reserved cream in a food processor or blender. Season with salt and pepper.

3 To make the salad, using a mandolin or sharp knife, very thinly slice the remaining 2 fennel bulbs. Combine the vinegar, fennel and 60ml (¼ cup) oil in a large bowl. Season with salt and pepper.

4 Heat 1½ tbs oil in a frying pan over high heat. Add half the prawns and cook for 1 minute on each side or until just cooked. Season. Repeat with remaining 1½ tbs oil and prawns.

5 Spoon fennel purée onto plates. Top with fennel salad and prawns. Scatter with reserved fennel fronds and drizzle prawn oil around the salad. Serve with grilled baguette.

TO FURTHER ENHANCE the flavour of the prawn oil, add 5 sprigs lemon thyme, 1 thinly sliced clove garlic, 1 bay leaf and 1 seeded, thinly sliced red bird's-eye chilli with the prawn shells in step 1. On the show, Claire blowtorched her prawns. If you have a blowtorch at home, you can quickly run it over the cooked prawns to sear them.

Claire won the chance to cook against chef Shaun Presland. The dish was an overwhelmingly tricky tuna tasting plate. With 10 minutes to go Claire almost gave up, but then summoned great willpower to put up a plate.

Alvin's CARAMELISED PORK BELLY WITH CHILLI VINEGAR

For the Seven Deadly Sins challenge Alvin chose Greed. This is a dish his mum makes: "Every time she cooks it I want more, so she cooks it in bulk!" The luxurious fattiness of the pork is cut by the vinegared chilli and lovely crisp ginger. The judges voted it "sensational".

8 cloves garlic, chopped
15 black peppercorns
Peanut oil, to fry
2.5L (10 cups) chicken stock
125ml (1/2 cup) Chinese rice wine (shaoxing)*
250ml cooking caramel (Karamel masakan)*
375ml (1 1/2 cups) light soy sauce

125ml (1/2 cup) oyster sauce
1 cinnamon quill
1 tsp ground star anise
1kg boneless pork belly
330g (1 1/2 cups) brown sugar
80ml (1/3 cup) fish sauce
2 tbs lime juice
5cm piece ginger, cut into julienne (matchsticks)

3 red eschalots, sliced
1 pinch saffron threads
400g (2 cups) jasmine rice, rinsed, drained
1 tbs black sesame seeds
1 long red chilli, thinly sliced
60ml (1/4 cup) rice wine vinegar
Coriander leaves, to garnish

1 Using a mortar and pestle, pound garlic and peppercorns to a paste. Heat 2 tbs peanut oil in a large saucepan over medium heat and fry paste for 2 minutes or until fragrant. Add 2L of stock, the wine, caramel, soy sauce, oyster sauce, cinnamon and star anise. Bring to the boil, then reduce heat to low. Add the pork belly and simmer, covered, for 1 hour. Remove the pork belly from the pan and set aside until cool enough to handle. Keep the braising liquid. Cut the pork into bite-sized pieces.

2 Fill a deep-fryer or large saucepan one-third full with peanut oil and heat over medium heat to 180°C (or until a cube of bread turns golden in 10 seconds). Working in small batches, gently drop the pork pieces into the oil and fry for 4 minutes or until golden. Drain on paper towel.

3 Preheat the oven to 60°C. Sprinkle the sugar into a large saucepan and cook over medium heat until the sugar starts to melt and caramelise. Carefully add 250ml (1 cup) of the braising liquid with the fish sauce and lime juice. Increase the heat to medium–high and cook for 5 minutes, or until reduced by one-third. Add the pork pieces, remove from the heat and keep warm.

4 Fill a small saucepan one-third full with oil and heat to 180°C (or until a cube of bread turns golden in 10 seconds). Cook the ginger until crisp. Remove with a slotted spoon and drain on paper towel. Repeat with the eschalots and reserve the oil.

5 Place 125ml (1/2 cup) of the reserved oil in a heatproof dish with the saffron threads and place into the oven for 20 minutes to infuse. Spoon 2 tbs of the saffron oil into a large saucepan. Add the rice and stir to coat. Add the remaining chicken stock, cover and cook over low heat for 20 minutes or until the rice has absorbed all the stock and is cooked. Fluff up the grains with a fork, transfer to a warm bowl and sprinkle with sesame seeds.

6 To serve, mix the sliced chilli and the vinegar in a small bowl. Sprinkle the pork with crisp eschalots, ginger and coriander leaves. Serve with the rice.

SHAOXING AND COOKING CARAMEL are available at Asian grocers. **FREEZE** leftover stock to use again.

Adam's ANGRY BIRD

Adam's Deadly Sin was Wrath and he immediately saw red. "I wanted to create different layers of heat and flavour that would start off sweet, move through savoury and finish hot. I used fresh chilli and black pepper for the spicy notes and honey, sugar, nashi pear and the sweetness from the chilli paste for the sweet notes. I think this is one of the best dishes I made in the competition... Gary even asked me for the recipe!"

1 x 1.6kg chicken, cut in 8 pieces
4 spring onions, finely chopped
1/2 red cabbage (375g), shredded
1 red onion, finely sliced
MARINADE
1 tbs sake
1 tbs soy sauce or tamari
1 tbs honey
1 tbs ground black pepper
1 tbs sesame oil
SAUCE
1/2 nashi pear, peeled, cored
1/2 onion

2 cloves garlic
1 tbs soy sauce or tamari
1 tbs sugar
2 tbs honey
1 tbs kochujan* (Korean chilli
    paste)
2 tbs chilli powder
2 bird's-eye chillies
1 tbs hot English mustard
1 tsp salt
PICKLED NASHI PEAR
60ml (1/4 cup) plum vinegar
60ml (1/4 cup) rice wine vinegar

1 tbs sugar
1 tsp salt
1 nashi pear, peeled, cut into 1cm
    dice
YUZU COLESLAW DRESSING
1 egg
60ml (1/4 cup) yuzu juice*
200ml olive oil
200ml peanut oil
1 tbs caster sugar
1 tsp salt

1 Place chicken in a large, shallow non-reactive dish. Mix together all marinade ingredients and pour over chicken, turning to coat. Marinate in fridge for 30 minutes.

2 Meanwhile, to make sauce, mix all the ingredients in a small food processor or blender until smooth. If too thick add a little water. Set aside.

3 To make pickled nashi pear, combine the vinegars, sugar and salt with 250ml (1 cup) water in a saucepan. Add the pear, cover with a round of baking paper to keep it submerged and cook over medium heat for 5 minutes or until just soft. Remove from heat, leave to cool and drain well.

4 To make yuzu coleslaw dressing, whisk egg and yuzu juice in a bowl. Whisking continuously, add the combined oils, drop by drop at first, then in a thin stream until thick. Season with the sugar and salt.

5 Preheat oven to 180°C. Heat a chargrill pan over high heat and cook chicken in batches until blackened all over. Place into a large ovenproof pan and cook for 10 minutes in the oven. Transfer to the stovetop and add the sauce. Cook over medium heat, turning to coat the chicken in the sauce, for 5 minutes or until the sauce darkens and thickens.

6 Arrange chicken on a platter and scatter with spring onions. Combine cabbage and red onion with coleslaw dressing and serve with the chicken, with pickled nashi pear on the side.

KOCHUJAN is available from Asian grocers. **YUZU** is a type of citrus fruit used in Japanese and Korean cookery. You will find the bottled juice in Asian grocers.

Serves **6**
Preparation **1 hour 15 minutes + overnight
refrigeration + 3 hours refrigeration**
Cooking **1 hour**

Callum's **CHOCOLATE DELICES**

Callum had a shocker of a morning with the mystery box, with George forcing him to taste his too-salty broth. "When George held up the spoon again and asked me to taste my Gluttony dish I almost had a heart attack." "Now taste something brilliant," said George.

55g (¼ cup) caster sugar
580ml (2⅓ cups) pouring cream
450g dark chocolate (70% cocoa
   solids), roughly chopped
5g leaf titanium-strength gelatine

1 egg, plus 1 egg yolk
Cocoa, freeze-dried raspberries,
   small mint leaves, to serve
ALMOND MACARONS
120g (1 cup) ground almonds

215g (1⅓ cups) icing sugar
3 egg whites
55g (¼ cup) caster sugar
¼ tsp cream of tartar
1 drop red food colouring

1 Cut six 6 x 20cm strips of baking paper and use to line six 6cm-deep, 6cm-wide ring moulds. Place moulds on a tray lined with baking paper.

2 To make caramel truffle base, place sugar and 1 tbs water in a small pan over high heat. Cook, without stirring, until a dark caramel. Gradually add 125ml (½ cup) cream and, using a metal spoon, stir until the caramel dissolves. Place 100g chocolate in a bowl, pour in hot cream mixture and stir until melted and combined. Pour into moulds. Chill for 30 minutes or until set.

3 To make chocolate mousse, place 150g chocolate in a heatproof bowl over a pan of gently simmering water. Stir until melted. Cool. Whisk 200ml cream to stiff peaks. Chill for 5 minutes to firm.

4 Soften gelatine in cold water for 3 minutes. Squeeze out excess water.

5 Place 100ml cream in a pan and slowly bring to the boil. Remove from heat and stir in gelatine until dissolved. Stir gelatine mixture, egg and egg yolk into melted chocolate until combined, then fold in the whipped cream. Spoon the chocolate mousse over the truffle bases, leaving a 3mm gap at the top of the moulds for the ganache. Refrigerate mousse overnight to set.

6 To make ganache, place remaining 155ml cream in a small saucepan and slowly bring to the boil. Place 100g chocolate in a bowl, pour in hot cream and stir until smooth. Pour ganache over the mousse and level the top with a knife. Chill for at least 3 hours to set.

7 To make chocolate curls, place the remaining 100g chocolate in a heatproof bowl over a pan of gently simmering water and stir until melted. Using a palette knife, spread chocolate 2mm thick onto a marble slab or an inverted clean metal tray and leave until almost set. Holding a large knife at a 45-degree angle, scrape chocolate away from you to create curls. Refrigerate until needed.

8 To make almond macarons, preheat oven to 120°C. Sift almonds with icing sugar 3 times. Using an electric mixer, whisk egg whites to soft peaks, then gradually add caster sugar, cream of tartar and colouring, and whisk to stiff peaks. Fold in the almond mixture until just combined (don't overmix). Spoon into a piping bag fitted with a 1cm plain nozzle and pipe 3cm rounds, 3cm apart onto 2 oven trays lined with baking paper (mixture makes 40). Leave for 20 minutes for a skin to form on macarons, then bake for 30 minutes or until macarons can be removed easily from trays. Remove from oven and leave macarons on trays to cool.

9 Run a hot knife around the inside of each mould to release délices, then slide off the moulds. Dust with cocoa and top with chocolate curls. Scatter freeze-dried (or frozen) raspberries, mint and more curls around délices and serve immediately with macarons.

Serves **6**
Preparation **3 hours**
Cooking 2½ **hours**

Courtney's TASTES OF CHINATOWN

For this last challenge before finals week there was time to plan, money to spend, four culinary-hero guests to impress and nowhere to hide. Now was the time to show some style.

MASTERSTOCK

2L (8 cups) low-salt chicken
  stock
150ml dark soy sauce
150ml light soy sauce
100ml Chinese rice wine
  (shaoxing)

2 star anise
1 cinnamon quill
¼ tsp Szechuan peppercorns
25g yellow rock sugar
½ tsp fennel seeds
2 pieces dried tangerine peel*

½ tsp white peppercorns
1cm piece ginger
1cm piece galangal
1 black cardamom pod

1 Combine all the ingredients in a large saucepan or stockpot. Bring to the boil, reduce the heat to low and simmer for 20 minutes.

SPATCHCOCK WITH FIVE-SPICE SALT

6 spatchcocks (450g each)
1 quantity masterstock, above
Vegetable oil, to deep-fry

2 tsp sea salt
1 tsp ground white pepper
1 tsp Chinese five-spice

½ tsp ground Szechuan
  peppercorns

1 Remove wishbones from spatchcocks. Place 3 spatchcocks in the masterstock and return to a simmer. Poach gently for 20 minutes. Carefully lift out with a large slotted spoon and sit upright to drain all liquid from the cavities. Poach remaining spatchcocks.* Pat dry and leave to cool completely. Reserve 250ml (1 cup) of the masterstock for the spiced broth.

2 Fill a deep fryer or large saucepan one-third full with the oil and heat over medium heat to 190°C (or until a cube of bread turns golden in 8 seconds). Gently lower the spatchcocks into the oil, 2 at a time, and cook, carefully turning to brown all sides, for 5 minutes or until dark golden. Lift out with a large slotted spoon and drain on paper towels. To serve, carve breast meat and legs. Keep the oil.

3 Using a mortar and pestle, finely grind seasonings to make five-spice salt.* Serve with spatchcocks.

DRIED TANGERINE PEEL is available in Asian food stores. **SPATCHCOCK** can be poached a few hours in advance and kept in the fridge. Fry close to serving time. **FIVE-SPICE SALT** can be made a day in advance.

"Courtney showed an amazing understanding of all the flavours and textures," said Kylie Kwong

SPICED BROTH

1L (4 cups) chicken stock
250ml (1 cup) masterstock,
   (page 222)
60ml (¼ cup) Chinese rice wine
   (shaoxing)
5 shiitake mushroom stems
2 red eschalots, peeled,
   quartered

2 cloves garlic, sliced
1cm piece ginger, sliced
2 tbs mirin
2 tbs light soy sauce
1 tbs honey
2 tsp rice vinegar
3 drops sesame oil
2 star anise

2 pieces dried tangerine peel
1 tsp bonito flakes
1 dried chilli
1 cinnamon quill
1 spring onion, thinly sliced
   diagonally

1 Place all the ingredients except spring onion in a large saucepan. Bring to the boil over medium–high heat, then reduce the heat to low and simmer for 45 minutes. Strain through a sieve to remove the solids and serve topped with the spring onions.*

SHIITAKE & LAP CHEONG OMELETTE

3 lap cheong (Chinese sausages),
   steamed for 10 minutes
1 tbs vegetable oil

5 fresh shiitake mushrooms,
   sliced
3 eggs

1 red eschalot, finely chopped

1 Cut the lap cheong into 5mm slices. Heat the oil in a non-stick frying pan and stir-fry lap cheong and mushrooms over medium heat for 5 minutes or until tender. Whisk the eggs with the eschalot and a pinch of salt and white pepper. Pour into the frying pan over the lap cheong and mushrooms. Cover and cook over low heat for 4 minutes or until set. Serve with XO eggplant sambal, below.

XO EGGPLANT SAMBAL

1 eggplant, cut into 2cm cubes
1 tbs salt
Vegetable oil, to deep-fry
1 tbs vegetable oil
1 red eschalot, finely chopped
1cm piece ginger, finely
   chopped

1 clove garlic, finely chopped
3 dried chillies, soaked for
   10 minutes, chopped
1 fresh chilli, chopped
2 tbs dried shrimp, soaked for
   10 minutes, chopped
2 tsp caster sugar

2 tsp Chinese rice wine
   (shaoxing)
1 tsp sesame oil
1 tbs light soy sauce

1 To make the sambal, sprinkle the eggplant generously with salt and leave for 10 minutes. Rinse well and drain. Pat dry with paper towels. Fill a saucepan one-third full with vegetable oil and cook the eggplant in 2 batches for 3 minutes or until dark golden. Drain on paper towels.

2 Heat the 1 tbs oil in a wok over medium heat and add the eschalot, ginger, garlic and a good pinch of salt. Stir-fry for 2 minutes, then add the soaked dried chillies, fresh chilli and shrimp. Stir-fry for 2 minutes. Stir in the sugar, wine and sesame oil and cook for 4 minutes or until the mixture turns dark golden. Toss through the eggplant and soy sauce and cook for 2 minutes or until well coated and heated through.

PORK & PRAWN DUMPLINGS

DUMPLINGS
100g pork mince
4 large green prawns, peeled, deveined, chopped
1 tsp chopped coriander
1cm piece ginger, finely chopped
1 small clove garlic, finely chopped

1 tsp finely chopped red eschalot
½ tsp caster sugar
1 pinch white pepper
1 tsp light soy sauce
3 drops sesame oil
12 gow gee wrappers
1 egg, lightly beaten

CHILLI SOY VINAIGRETTE*
1 tbs light soy sauce
2 tsp dark soy sauce
2 tsp rice wine vinegar
1 red chilli, chopped
½ tsp caster sugar
3 drops sesame oil
2 drops chilli oil

1 To make the dumplings, mix all ingredients except wrappers and egg. Lay out the wrappers and divide the filling evenly among them **(PIC 1)**. Brush around filling with egg. Gather the wrapper around the filling **(PIC 2)**, pinching to seal and form a small pouch.* Cook in a large bamboo steamer lined with baking paper, making sure they aren't touching, for 18 minutes, or until cooked through.

2 To make the chilli soy vinaigrette, mix together all ingredients. Serve with the dumplings.

SESAME & CUCUMBER SALAD

125ml (½ cup) rice wine vinegar
110g (½ cup) caster sugar
1 tsp sea salt
1 large cucumber, peeled, seeded, cut into julienne (matchsticks)

3cm piece daikon, cut into julienne (matchsticks)
½ tsp each toasted black and white sesame seeds
Micro herbs, to serve

DRESSING*
1 tbs oil
1 tsp Dijon mustard
1 tbs rice wine vinegar
2 tsp caster sugar
3 drops sesame oil

1 Combine vinegar, sugar, salt and 125ml (½ cup) warm water in a non-reactive bowl. Add the cucumber and daikon and leave for 30 minutes. Drain.

2 Whisk all dressing ingredients with a pinch of salt. Drizzle over salad with sesame seeds and herbs.

SPICED BROTH can be made a few hours in advance and kept in the fridge. Reheat close to serving time. **UNCOOKED DUMPLINGS** can be made a few hours in advance and kept in the fridge, covered with plastic wrap on a tray lined with baking paper. Steam close to serving time. **CHILLI SOY VINAIGRETTE** and **DRESSING FOR SESAME AND CUCUMBER SALAD** can be made a day in advance.

Adam's SEVEN LUCKY GODS OF JAPAN

The best four signature dishes of the culinary-hero challenge would take their cooks straight to finals week. Would Adam's lucky gods look favourably upon him?

EBISU (God of Fishing and Good Fortune)
TUNA WITH AVOCADO & YUZU MAYONNAISE

300g sashimi-grade tuna

1 tbs undrained pickled ginger

1 egg

1 tsp caster sugar

2 tbs yuzu juice

300ml grape seed oil

¹/₂ avocado, chopped

1 Cut tuna into long strips, 2cm wide and 2cm thick. Season well. Heat a yakitori grill or barbecue hotplate over high heat and sear tuna for a few seconds on each side. Remove, cover and refrigerate.

2 To make mayonnaise, drain ginger, keeping 1 tbs of liquid. Blend liquid, egg, sugar and yuzu juice in a blender or small processor. With the motor running, gradually add oil, drop by drop at first, then in a thin steady stream until thick and emulsified. Add avocado and blend. Season with salt and white pepper, cover surface with plastic wrap and refrigerate for no more than 30 minutes before serving.

3 To serve, slice the tuna and thread 2-3 pieces onto each of 6 small soaked* bamboo skewers. Serve with pickled ginger and mayonnaise.

BENZAITEN (Goddess of Music and Art)
SCALLOPS WITH ASIAN SALSA VERDE & TURMERIC OIL

200ml grape seed oil

¹/₂ onion, diced

2 tbs ground turmeric

1 tsp chilli powder

1 tsp salt

6 large scallops, cleaned, roe
   removed

ASIAN SALSA VERDE

¹/₂ cup coriander leaves

¹/₂ cup mint leaves

1 tbs fish sauce

1 tbs light soy sauce

2 long green chillies, halved
   lengthwise, seeded

1 clove garlic, roughly chopped

1 tbs yuzu juice

1 tbs rice wine vinegar

1 tsp caster sugar

6 shiso (perilla) leaves

1 Combine oil, onion, turmeric, chilli powder and salt in a small saucepan. Cook, stirring, over low–medium heat for 5 minutes or until onion is soft. Using a deep-frying thermometer, maintain oil temperature between 100°C and 122°C and continute cooking for 35 minutes. Cool and strain.

2 To make Asian salsa verde, combine herbs, sauces, chillies, garlic, yuzu juice, vinegar, sugar and shiso leaves in a small food processor and mix to a rough paste. Cover and refrigerate until required.

3 Thread one scallop onto each of 6 small soaked* bamboo skewers. Heat a yakitori or barbecue grill over high heat and sear scallops for 30 seconds on each side. Serve with salsa verde and turmeric oil.

Adam's SEVEN LUCKY GODS OF JAPAN

DAIDOKUTEN (God of Harvest and the Kitchen)
SHIITAKE MUSHROOMS, ASPARAGUS TIPS & LEMON

6 large fresh shiitake mushrooms
  with thick stems
6 asparagus tips (3–4cm long)

Vegetable oil, to brush
1 thin slice lemon, cut into
  6 triangles

1 Remove stalks from mushroom caps **(PIC 1)** and trim any woody ends from stalks **(PIC 2)**. Thread a stalk and cap onto each of 6 small soaked* bamboo skewers. Brush the mushroom skewers and asparagus tips with oil and season with salt.

2 Heat a yakitori or barbecue grill over high heat and grill the mushrooms for 2 minutes on each side. Grill the asparagus tips, turning frequently, for 3 minutes or until charred but still crunchy. Serve each skewer with an asparagus tip and lemon triangle.

HOTEI (Chinese God of Contentment and Happiness)
PORK BELLY WITH GREEN TEA SALT & SZECHUAN PEPPER

2 tsp green tea powder (matcha)
3 tsp sea salt

2 tsp Szechuan peppercorns
250g boneless pork belly

1 Using a mortar and pestle, grind the green tea and salt to a fine powder. Toast the peppercorns in a small frying pan over medium heat for 2 minutes or until fragrant. Grind in a spice grinder or with a mortar and pestle to a fine powder.

2 Cut the pork into 1cm-thick slices, then cut each slice into 3cm lengths. Thread 3 pieces of pork lengthwise onto each of 6 small soaked* bamboo skewers and lightly season. Heat an oiled yakitori or barbecue grill over high heat and grill the skewers for 8 minutes or until golden, turning occasionally. Serve scattered with green tea salt and ground pepper.

JUROJIN (God of Longevity)
SOUSED VENISON UMEJISO

200g venison fillet
60ml (¼ cup) sake

1 tsp ground white pepper
6 shiso (perilla) leaves

2 salted plums (umeboshi), finely
  chopped

1 Finely slice the venison and place in a non-reactive bowl with the sake and pepper. Cover and marinate for 30 minutes. Drain venison and season with salt.

2 Thread venison onto 6 small soaked* bamboo skewers. Heat a yakitori or barbecue grill over high heat and grill the venison for 3 minutes, or until medium–rare, turning once during cooking. Serve venison on shiso leaves with salted plums.

BISHAMONTEN (God of War and Warriors)

WAGYU SHORT RIB WITH WASABI & PEA SHOOTS

| 400g wagyu beef short rib | 2 tsp wasabi paste, or to taste | ⅓ cup pea shoots |

1 Trim the bones and excess fat from the ribs and cut the meat into 2cm cubes. Thread the meat onto 6 small soaked* bamboo skewers and season well with salt and white pepper. Heat an oiled yakitori or barbecue grill over high heat and grill the beef for 3 minutes on each side for medium–rare.

2 To serve, spread a little wasabi onto the beef on each skewer and serve scattered with pea shoots.

FUKUROKUJU (God of Wisdom)

CHICKEN & LEEK SKEWERS WITH SEVEN-SPICE PEPPER

125ml (½ cup) soy sauce	1 tsp dashi powder	3 chicken thigh fillets, cut into
2 tbs sake	1 tbs molasses (optional)	3cm pieces
60ml (¼ cup) mirin	1 tsp arrowroot	Shichimi togarashi (Japanese
55g (¼ cup) sugar	2 leeks, white part only	seven-spice pepper), to serve

1 Combine soy sauce, sake, mirin, sugar, dashi and molasses in a saucepan. Stir over low heat to dissolve sugar, then bring to a simmer. Dissolve arrowroot in 60ml (¼ cup) cold water and add to the saucepan. Cook, stirring, for 1–2 minutes until the sauce is thickened and glossy. Set aside to cool and transfer to a tall glass or jug so skewers can be dipped into the sauce.

2 Cut away the tough outer leaves of the leek and use only the tender white centre core of about 2cm diameter **(PIC 3)**. Cut into 3cm lengths. Thread 1 piece of leek onto each of 6 small soaked* bamboo skewers. Follow with 2 pieces of chicken. Add another piece of leek to finish.

3 Heat an oiled yakitori or barbecue grill over high heat. Dip the skewers into the sauce and grill. Continue to dip the skewers into the sauce throughout cooking (or baste with a pastry brush). Cook for 5 minutes on each side or until charred and cooked through. Serve with seven-spice pepper.

SOAK BAMBOO SKEWERS in cold water for 20 minutes before use to prevent them burning.

The judging panel was made up of four culinary greats: Kylie Kwong, Alla Wolf-Tasker, Mark Best and Jacques Reymond.

Serves **4**
Preparation **50 minutes**
Cooking **40 minutes**

Alvin's FISH & CHIPS WITH CUCUMBER SALSA

The name-that-fish elimination round was an anxious time for Alvin. "After a dismal performance in round 1, when I couldn't identify a flathead (despite its having a flat head), I was certain I would be eliminated. My place in the Top 6 was to be determined by fish and chips, something I had never made before. Gary said he wanted crunch, so I took that advice seriously. After all, why batter OR crumb, when you can batter AND crumb?" It meant home-time for Aaron, but he left as he would have hoped – like a rock star.

4 russet or sebago potatoes, cut into 1.5cm thick chips	**BATTER**	¼ red onion, diced
	225g (1½ cups) plain flour	1 tbs finely chopped flat-leaf parsley
Peanut oil, to deep-fry	1 tsp sweet paprika	
8 flathead fillets (about 600g)	1 tsp chilli powder	1 tsp vinegar
150g (2 cups) Japanese panko breadcrumbs	375ml (1½ cups) cold beer	1 tsp lemon juice
	CUCUMBER SALSA	1 pinch of sugar
Lemon wedges, to serve	1 Lebanese cucumber, diced	1 tbs olive oil

1 To make batter, sift the flour, paprika and chilli powder into a bowl and make a well in the centre. Add the beer gradually, whisking until smooth (batter should have the consistency of pouring cream). Cover with plastic wrap and leave for 20 minutes.

2 Place potatoes in a large saucepan, cover with cold water and bring to the boil over high heat. Cook for 10 minutes or until just tender. Drain well and spread out in a single layer on a tray to dry out and to cool slightly.

3 To make the salsa, combine all the ingredients in a bowl and adjust seasonings to taste – the salsa should be sour but slightly sweet.

4 Fill a deep-fryer or large saucepan one-third full with oil and heat over medium heat to 130°C (or until a cube of bread turns golden in 15 seconds). Deep-fry the chips in 3 batches for 3 minutes. Remove with a slotted spoon and drain on paper towels. Increase heat to 180°C (or until a cube of bread turns golden in 10 seconds). Return chips to the pan and cook for a further 7 minutes or until golden. Drain on paper towels and keep warm.

5 Working in 3 batches, dip the flathead fillets in batter, letting excess drain off. Coat with bread-crumbs. Gently drop into the oil and fry, turning halfway, for 3 minutes or until crisp and golden. Remove with a slotted spoon and drain on paper towels. Serve with chips, salsa and lemon wedges.

Alvin's grandfather's yam cakes sent him to the elimination test. Yams weren't to be found in the pantry so he improvised with swedes. It soon became clear that his grandfather had used yams for a good reason.

Chapter Six

THE FINAL DASH

It's finals week and the house is getting emptier. The V8 Cake ruthlessly dispatches Alvin. Jimmy chooses the ingredients for the "mystery box from hell", and Courtney says goodbye, again. Maggie Beer judges cookbook ideas, the Top 3 cook for the G-G and a mountain of lamb defeats Claire. Adam and Callum create their final MasterChef masterpieces.

Callum's LENTIL CURRY WITH FLAT BREADS

"Jimmy, what are we cooking?" Jimmy won the Adriano Zumbo V8 pressure test and was given the prize of choosing the 12 mystery box ingredients. The Top 5 – Adam, Callum, Claire, Jimmy and Courtney – all created one savoury and one sweet dish from his box of difficult spicy tricks. "This challenge could swing wildly from brilliant to terrible," said Gary.

150g (3/4 cup) red lentils
1 onion, chopped
3 garlic cloves, finely chopped
3cm piece ginger, finely chopped
2 bird's-eye chillies, finely chopped
1 1/2 tsp garam masala

1 tbs curry powder
2 tbs vegetable oil
2 large vine-ripened tomatoes, chopped
1/2 lemon, juiced
Plain yoghurt, coriander and sliced chilli, to serve

FLAT BREADS
200g (1 1/3 cups) plain flour
2 tbs pouring cream
Vegetable oil, to fry

1 Rinse the lentils in a sieve under cold water until the water runs clear. Soak the lentils in 680ml (2 3/4 cups) water until needed.

2 Combine the onion, garlic, ginger, chillies, garam masala, curry powder and oil in a small food processor and process to a paste. Transfer to a saucepan and cook over very low heat for 3 minutes or until fragrant. Add a little more oil if sticking, taking care not to burn the paste.

3 Add the tomatoes and lemon juice to the pan and cook, stirring often, for 10 minutes or until the tomatoes have broken down. Add the lentils and water and bring to the boil. Reduce the heat to low–medium and cook, stirring often, for a further 20 minutes or until the lentils are tender.

4 Meanwhile, to make flat breads, put the flour and cream in a food processor. Using the pulse button, process in short bursts until combined. Add 80ml (1/3 cup) water and pulse until the dough comes together. Turn out onto a lightly floured surface and knead for 10 minutes or until smooth and silky. Wrap in plastic wrap and rest for 20 minutes.

5 Roll the dough into a sausage shape, then cut into 8 equal portions. Roll out the portions on a lightly floured surface to rounds 2mm thick. Heat a frying pan over medium heat and brush lightly with oil. Cook the flat breads for 1 minute on each side or until slightly puffed and golden.

6 Season the curry well and serve with the flat breads, yoghurt, coriander and sliced chilli.

"I've been making a lot of curries in the house with Jimmy recently, but I don't know if it's a good idea to try to out-curry him."
Callum won the challenge, so it wasn't a bad idea.

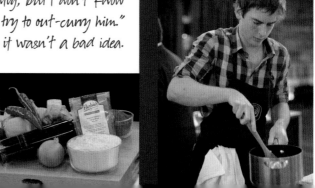

Serves **8**
Preparation **40 minutes**
+ 1 hour refrigeration
Cooking **35 minutes**

Callum's LEMON AND GINGER BRULEE TARTS

Guest judge Shannon Bennett was impressed with Callum's dessert. "It's got a homemade feel and a Frenchiness about it that I like. The pastry's really delicate." Gary was also smitten: "The reason I'm the shape I am is because, when confronted with a dessert like this, it's very hard for me to stop eating." Matt offered help: "Gary, step away from the pastry!"

260g (1¾ cups) plain flour
40g (¼ cup) icing sugar
150g cold unsalted butter, chopped
1 egg, lightly beaten

FILLING
300ml pouring cream
200ml milk
2 lemons, zested
6cm piece ginger, thinly sliced

5 egg yolks
75g (⅓ cup) caster sugar
1 tbs cornflour
75g (⅓ cup) caster sugar

1 Preheat the oven to 180°C. Grease eight 8cm tart pans with removable bases. Put the flour, icing sugar and butter in a food processor and, using the pulse button, process in short bursts until the mixture resembles breadcrumbs. Add the egg and pulse until the dough begins to come together. Turn out onto a lightly floured surface and gather the dough together.

2 Divide the dough into 8 equal portions and roll out on a lightly floured surface until 3mm thick. Line the pans with the pastry and refrigerate for 30 minutes.

3 Prick the pastry bases with a fork and line each with baking paper. Fill with dried beans or uncooked rice and place on large oven trays. Bake for 15 minutes, then remove the paper and beans and bake for a further 10 minutes or until lightly golden. Cool completely.

4 To make filling, mix cream, milk, lemon zest and ginger in a saucepan and bring almost to the boil. Remove from the heat and leave for 5 minutes for the flavours to infuse. Whisk the egg yolks, sugar and cornflour in a bowl until thick and pale. Pour the infused milk slowly into the egg yolk mixture, whisking continuously. Strain through a sieve into a clean saucepan and stir over low–medium heat for 3 minutes or until the mixture thickens and begins to simmer. Remove from the heat.

5 Leave to cool slightly for 5 minutes, then spoon into the tart cases and smooth the surface. Refrigerate for 30 minutes.

6 Sprinkle the surface of each tart with 2 tsp caster sugar and use a kitchen blowtorch to caramelise the sugar. Leave for 5 minutes to cool and set.

The "mystery box from hell" caused problems for everyone, including its mastermind, Jimmy. Courtney just couldn't think of a dessert she could cook with all those spices.

Claire's SCALLOPS WITH TOFFEED APPLE

The Top 4 took part in the cookbook challenge. They each had 2½ hours to cook three dishes that would appear in their own book of recipes. Guest judge Maggie Beer wanted to have all her senses engaged and to see food that was "genuine, original and true to yourself". The Final 4 were all so very different, but all leapt at this chance to shine.

1 small granny smith apple
1 tbs lemon juice
8 scallops
1 tbs olive oil
Micro cress, to serve

TOFFEED APPLE
110g (½ cup) caster sugar
1 granny smith apple, peeled,
  cored, diced
SAUCE
80ml (⅓ cup) Calvados

2 tbs apple cider vinegar
2 eschalots, chopped
2 cloves garlic, finely chopped
80g butter, cubed

1 To make the toffeed apple, preheat the oven to 180°C. Combine the sugar and 50ml water in a saucepan and stir over low heat to dissolve the sugar. Bring to the boil and cook over medium heat until caramelised. Arrange the diced apple on an oven tray lined with baking paper and pour the toffee over the apple. Bake in the oven for 5 minutes or until the apple is tender and caramelised.

2 To make the sauce, combine the Calvados, vinegar, eschalots and garlic in a small saucepan. Bring to the boil over medium heat and cook for 3 minutes or until reduced by two-thirds. Strain into a clean pan over low heat and whisk in the butter a little at a time until smooth and emulsified. Set aside and keep warm.

3 Cut the cheeks from the apple, then cut into matchsticks. Place in a bowl of cold water with the lemon juice added.

4 Heat a large frying pan over high heat. Toss the scallops in a little olive oil and season with salt and pepper. Cook for 30–60 seconds on each side (depending on thickness) or until opaque. Drizzle with 60ml (¼ cup) of the sauce and toss to coat.

5 Drain the apple and toss with the micro cress. Drizzle with 2 tbs of the sauce. Spoon onto plates and top with a scallop. Spoon a little toffeed apple on top.

"I'm not one for gratuitous public displays of affection, but I just want to give Maggie Beer a big hug," said Claire.

Claire's RARE ROAST BEEF WITH DAUPHINOISE POTATOES & RED WINE JUS

This was a very personal challenge for Claire. She dreams of opening a country restaurant called Hearth, so *Cooking from the Hearth* was her book title. The theme: "honest, timeless food that reflects the warmth of the big central fireplace and makes you feel loved." On the day, Claire's jus didn't work well, but she's perfected it for this recipe.

600g piece sirloin steak (such as wagyu), at room temperature
2 tbs olive oil
2 slices bone marrow, optional
RED WINE JUS
375ml (1½ cups) red wine
375ml (1½ cups) veal stock
125ml (½ cup) port
4 eschalots, thinly sliced

5 Swiss brown mushrooms (100g), thinly sliced
3 sprigs thyme
1 bay leaf
50g cold butter, chopped
DAUPHINOISE POTATOES
4 waxy potatoes (such as nicola), peeled, thinly sliced*
8 black peppercorns

4 cloves garlic, chopped
3 sprigs thyme
1 bay leaf
1 whole nutmeg
625ml (2½ cups) pouring cream

1 To make red wine jus, combine the red wine, veal stock, port, eschalots, mushrooms, thyme and bay leaf in a saucepan. Bring to the boil, reduce the heat to low–medium and simmer for 25 minutes or until reduced by two-thirds. Strain, return to the pan over low–medium heat and whisk in the butter a little at a time until smooth. Season to taste and keep warm.

2 For the potatoes, preheat the oven to 200°C. Arrange the potatoes in a large deep frying pan. Add the peppercorns, garlic, thyme and bay leaf. Finely grate ¾ of the nutmeg into the pan and season with salt. Pour the cream over the potatoes. Bring to the boil, reduce the heat to medium and cook for 3 minutes or until just tender but still firm. Cool slightly and drain potatoes, reserving the cream.

3 Arrange the potatoes in layers in 4 ring moulds* (10cm diameter x 3cm deep) on an oven tray lined with baking paper. Spoon a little cream between the potato as you layer. Cover with lightly oiled foil and bake for 25 minutes or until the potatoes are tender when tested with a small sharp knife. Remove the foil and cook under a medium–hot grill for 5 minutes or until crisp and golden.

4 To roast the beef, increase the oven to 220°C. Heat a large ovenproof frying pan over high heat. Season the oil with salt and rub into the meat. Sear the meat in the hot pan until well caramelised on all sides. Transfer the pan to the oven and cook for 12 minutes or until the internal temperature of the meat is 46°C when tested with a meat thermometer. Transfer the meat to a warm plate and rest for 10 minutes before cutting into thin slices.

5 To serve, heat the marrow in the oven for 1-2 minutes or until soft. Remove the potato from the ring moulds and arrange on plates. Top with the roast beef and marrow and serve immediately with warm red wine jus.

IF YOU HAVE A MANDOLIN, use it to slice the potatoes. **COOK THE POTATOES** in a baking dish or individual ramekins if you don't have small ring moulds.

"This beef is melt-in-the-mouth." Maggie Beer

Serves **4**
Preparation **30 minutes**
+ 6 hours refrigeration
Cooking **30 minutes**

Claire's ORANGE BLOSSOM PANNA COTTA WITH PAIN PERDU & BLOOD ORANGE SYRUP

Matt Preston waxed lyrical about Claire's cookbook dessert. "If I was Julie Andrews and this was *The Sound of Music*, I'd be singing a song about my favourite things... and they'd be French toast, the flavour of blood orange, panna cotta and that beautiful smell of orange blossom. I love this. It's a great dessert."

45g (1 cup) kataifi pastry*
PANNA COTTA
200ml milk
55g (¼ cup) caster sugar
3½ leaves gold-strength
  gelatine
200ml pouring cream
3 tsp orange blossom water

BLOOD ORANGE SYRUP
180ml (¾ cup) freshly squeezed
  blood orange juice,* strained
55g (¼ cup) caster sugar
PAIN PERDU
160ml (⅔ cup) milk
1 vanilla bean, split, seeds
  scraped

160ml (⅔ cup) pouring cream
3 egg yolks
2 tbs caster sugar
4 thick slices day-old brioche
2 tbs ghee

1 To make the panna cotta, mix milk and sugar in a small saucepan and stir over low–medium heat for 2 minutes or until sugar has dissolved. Meanwhile, soften the gelatine in cold water for 3 minutes, then squeeze out the excess water. Add to the pan and stir to dissolve. Mix together cream, orange blossom water and hot milk mixture until well combined. Pour into four 125ml (½-cup) dariole moulds* and refrigerate for 6 hours or until set.

2 Preheat the oven to 200°C and line an oven tray with baking paper. Divide the kataifi pastry into 4 small piles on the tray. Spray with oil and bake for 15 minutes or until crisp and golden.

3 To make blood orange syrup, mix the orange juice and sugar in a small saucepan and stir over low heat without boiling until the sugar has dissolved. Increase the heat to medium, bring to the boil and cook for 5 minutes or until reduced and syrupy.

4 To make pain perdu, mix milk, vanilla bean and seeds, and cream in a small saucepan. Bring just to a simmer over low heat. Whisk together the egg yolks and sugar in a large bowl until thick and pale. Pour the hot cream mixture onto the egg mixture, whisking continuously. Discard the vanilla bean.

5 Lay the brioche in a single layer in a large shallow dish. Pour half the custard over the brioche and leave for 2 minutes to soak. Turn the brioche, pour over remaining custard and leave to soak again.

6 Just before serving, melt the ghee in a large frying pan over low heat. Lift brioche out of custard and fry for 2 minutes each side until golden (watch carefully so it doesn't burn). Keep warm.

7 Pour blood orange syrup into 4 shallow bowls. Place pain perdu in each bowl. Carefully turn the panna cotta out of the dariole moulds and place on top of pain perdu. Top with kataifi pastry.

KATAIFI PASTRY is a finely shredded filo-like pastry used in Greek or Middle Eastern sweets. It is available from specialist food shops and some delis. **BLOOD ORANGES** have beautiful crimson juice but a short season, so use navel or Valencia oranges if necessary. **DARIOLE MOULDS** are small cup-like moulds made from metal or plastic.

Serves **6**
Preparation **30 minutes**
Cooking **40 minutes**

Callum's COCONUT MUSSELS

Maggie Beer found this dish "exciting, fresh and alive", but Matt Preston thought it a little too salty. Callum had forgotten that the juices released when the mussels opened would add more salt to the dish. In Asian cooking the balance of flavours is all-important, so taste often and adjust the seasoning with fish sauce after the mussels have opened.

1L low-salt chicken stock
60ml (¼ cup) lime juice
2 tbs palm sugar
1 tbs fish sauce
270ml can coconut milk
1.25kg mussels, scrubbed, beards removed

Coriander leaves and shredded spring onions, to serve
CURRY PASTE
2 red eschalots, chopped
2 cloves garlic, chopped
2 bird's-eye chillies, chopped
5 coriander roots, chopped

5cm piece ginger, chopped
5cm piece turmeric, chopped
1 tbs ground coriander
1 tsp ground turmeric
1 tbs shrimp paste
2 tbs vegetable oil

1 To make the curry paste, process all the ingredients in a small food processor until almost smooth.
2 Heat a large saucepan over low heat. Add the curry paste and cook, stirring, for 5 minutes or until aromatic. Add a little more oil if sticking, taking care not to burn the paste.
3 Stir in the stock and 500ml (2 cups) water. Increase heat to high and bring to the boil. Reduce heat to low and simmer for 30 minutes or until reduced by half. Add lime juice, palm sugar and half the fish sauce, stirring to dissolve the sugar.
4 Stir in the coconut milk. Strain through a sieve to remove any coarse pieces. Wipe the saucepan clean with paper towel and return liquid to the saucepan. Bring to the boil over high heat.
5 Add the mussels to the pan, cover and cook, stirring occasionally, for 4 minutes or until the mussels have opened. Taste the sauce and adjust for correct balance of lime juice, fish sauce and sugar, adding the rest of the fish sauce if necessary. Serve the mussels with the sauce, topped with coriander leaves and spring onions.

Callum's cookbook idea was A Cook's Roadmap, featuring chapters on different cooking techniques, such as braising and confit. This recipe demonstrates a simple curry paste and perfectly cooked mussels.

Serves **8**

Preparation **1 hour + 1½ hours**
refrigeration **+ 2 hours freezing**
Cooking **15–20 minutes**

Callum's CHOCOLATE FONDANTS WITH ORANGE DATE ICE-CREAM

ORANGE DATE ICE-CREAM
6 egg yolks
75g (⅓ cup) caster sugar
300ml pouring cream
250ml (1 cup) milk
2 oranges, zested
1 tbs dried orange peel*
20g pitted dates, diced

SESAME TUILE BISCUITS
50g unsalted butter, melted
  and cooled
55g (¼ cup) caster sugar
50ml egg whites
50g (⅓ cup) plain flour
1 tsp sesame seeds

FONDANTS
200g dark couverture chocolate,
  chopped
165g unsalted butter, chopped
4 eggs
4 egg yolks
110g (½ cup) caster sugar
100g (⅔ cup) plain flour, sifted

1 To make ice-cream, whisk egg yolks and sugar in a large bowl until thick and pale. Put cream, milk, orange zest and peel in a saucepan and bring just to the boil. Remove from heat and pour into the egg yolk mixture, whisking continuously. Pour back into the saucepan and stir over low heat for 5 minutes or until custard coats the back of a spoon. Strain through a sieve into a bowl over a bowl of ice and stir for 2 minutes to cool. Transfer to an ice-cream maker and churn for 15 minutes. Add the dates and churn for a further 15 minutes or until smooth and frozen. Freeze for 2 hours or until firm.

2 To make sesame tuile biscuits, preheat oven to 170°C and line a large oven tray with baking paper. Mix butter and sugar in a bowl, then stir in the egg whites. Fold in the flour. Spread mixture paper-thin onto tray to make a 25 x 35cm rectangle and sprinkle with sesame seeds. Bake for 5 minutes or until golden. Working quickly, use a 5cm round cutter to cut out 16 biscuits. Cool on tray. Store in an airtight container until required.

3 To make fondants, line a large heavy-based oven tray* with baking paper. Grease nine* 6cm-diameter, 6cm-deep ring moulds with butter. Line with baking paper, avoiding creases and ensuring paper is stuck to the rings so fondants unmould easily. Put 1 mould on a separate tray to test cooking time.

4 Fill a saucepan one-third full with water and bring to a gentle simmer. Place chocolate and butter in a heatproof bowl over pan and stir until melted (don't let the bowl touch the water).

5 Meanwhile, beat eggs, egg yolks and sugar in a large bowl with an electric mixer until thick and pale. Fold one-third of the egg mixture into the chocolate to loosen, then fold all chocolate mixture into egg mixture in 2 batches. Gently fold in flour in 2 batches. Pour into the ring moulds. Refrigerate for at least 45 minutes or until required.

6 About 20 minutes before serving, preheat oven to 180°C. Bake test fondant for 12 minutes to check cooking time, then cool for 2 minutes on tray. Fondant should have a gooey centre. Cook remaining fondants, adding or reducing cooking time by 2 minutes if necessary. Allow to cool for 2 minutes on tray. Carefully lift off ring moulds, unpeeling the baking paper. Transfer fondants to plates. Serve with a scoop of the ice-cream sandwiched between 2 tuile biscuits.

DRIED ORANGE PEEL is available from the spice section of specialist food shops. **THE OVEN TRAY** must be flat and heavy duty so it doesn't buckle during cooking, causing mixture to leak. **THE FONDANT MIXTURE** makes 9. This lets you cook one first, as Callum did, to check the timing, which can vary between ovens.

"Jonathan, Matthew and I spent a lot of time in the house discussing what makes a great fondant... that perfect balance of just-set crust and gooey molten centre." Callum

Adam's SMOKED KINGFISH CHIRASHI ZUSHI

275g sashimi-grade tuna
Salmon roe and micro herbs,
  to serve
SUSHI RICE
300g (1½ cups) sushi rice
100ml rice wine vinegar
2 tbs caster sugar
½ tsp salt
YUZU JELLY
50ml yuzu juice
1½ tsp agar agar powder
½ tsp bicarbonate of soda

MATCHA JELLY
½ tsp green tea powder
1½ tsp agar agar powder
SMOKED KINGFISH
200g kingfish fillet, skinned, cut
  into 1.5cm slices
2 tbs brown sugar
2 tbs dried mandarin or orange
  peel
2 tbs hickory chips
1 tbs earl grey tea leaves

OMELETTE
2 eggs
1 tsp caster sugar
1 tsp dashi powder
SHIITAKE MUSHROOMS
6 dried shiitake mushrooms,
  soaked in hot water for
  15 minutes, drained
100ml light soy sauce
2 tbs caster sugar
2 tbs sake
2 tbs mirin

1 To make sushi rice, rinse rice under cold running water for 2 minutes or until water runs clear; drain. Transfer to a rice cooker, add 375ml (1½ cups) water and cook according to manufacturer's instructions. Leave to stand for 10 minutes. Combine rice wine vinegar, sugar and salt in a small bowl and stir until dissolved. Brush a large shallow non-reactive bowl with some of the seasoned vinegar. Put rice in bowl and sprinkle with most of the seasoned vinegar. Using a rice paddle or large wooden spoon, turn the rice continuously to cool and coat it in the seasoned vinegar, fanning with other hand to cool it quickly at the same time. Continue turning and fanning until rice cools to blood temperature. Dip a muslin cloth in remaining seasoned vinegar and cover rice until ready to use.

2 To make yuzu jelly, lightly grease a 16 x 26cm baking pan and line with plastic freezer paper. Whisk all ingredients with 200ml water in a small saucepan. Bring to the boil over medium–high heat, whisking continuously. Reduce heat slightly and simmer for 2 minutes or until slightly thickened. Pour into lined tray and refrigerate for 20 minutes or until set. Cut into 5mm cubes.

3 To make matcha jelly, whisk ingredients with 250ml (1 cup) water and repeat step 2 with another tray.

4 To make smoked kingfish, put kingfish slices on a lightly oiled wire rack. Line a wok with foil and place sugar, mandarin peel, hickory chips and tea leaves on foil. Heat wok over high heat until smoking. Turn off heat and place rack of kingfish over smoking mixture. Cover tightly with a lid or foil and leave to smoke for 5 minutes. Remove from wok, cover and refrigerate until ready to serve.

5 To make omelette, whisk all ingredients together. Lightly oil a non-stick frying pan and heat over medium heat. Pour in half the mixture, swirling to coat pan. Cook until set, then remove, roll up and slice thinly. Repeat with remaining mixture.

6 Thinly slice shiitake mushrooms. Place in a small saucepan with remaining ingredients and bring to the boil. Reduce heat to medium and simmer for 10 minutes or until all liquid has evaporated.

7 Cut tuna into 2cm lengths and season well. Heat a barbecue plate or non-stick frying pan over high heat and sear tuna for 2 seconds on all sides. Remove from pan and refrigerate for 10 minutes.

8 Thinly slice kingfish and cut tuna into slices. Place a mound of rice in each bowl, scatter with the jellies, kingfish, omelette, mushrooms, tuna, roe and herbs.

Serves **4**
Preparation **20 minutes**
+ **4 hours refrigeration**
Cooking **40 minutes**

Jimmy's **CHAI LATTE CREME BRULEE**

Although Jimmy went home after the cookbook challenge, his chai crème brûlée was one of the favourites dishes. On the day, his mixture didn't set properly, but the flavour was a delight and George scraped his bowl clean. Jimmy remembers that the idea came from a casual comment in the MasterChef house: "I used to make chai tea for everyone at bedtime... It started as a massive pot and got smaller as the number of contestants fell. One night Callum and I thought, 'this tastes so good, why don't we make it into a dessert?'"

600ml thickened cream
¼ tsp ground cardamom
1 vanilla bean, split, seeds
 scraped

6 egg yolks
55g (¼ cup) caster sugar
60g demerara sugar, to
 caramelise tops

Ground cinnamon,
 to dust

1 Preheat oven to 120°C. Put the cream, cardamom, vanilla bean and seeds in a saucepan over medium heat and bring almost to the boil, then remove from heat. Remove vanilla bean and discard.
2 Whisk together the egg yolks and caster sugar in a bowl for 2 minutes or until thick and pale. Pour the hot cream over the egg yolk mixture, whisking continuously until well combined. Strain into a jug and pour into four 200ml ramekins.
3 Carefully place ramekins in a deep roasting pan lined with a folded tea towel. Pour boiling water into the pan to come halfway up the sides of ramekins. Cover the whole pan loosely with foil.
4 Bake in the oven for 40 minutes or until the custards are just set. Remove ramekins from the roasting pan and set aside to cool. Refrigerate for at least 4 hours.
5 Sprinkle demerara sugar evenly over the baked custards. Use a kitchen blowtorch to caramelise the sugar. If you don't have a blowtorch, place custards in a roasting pan packed with ice, then place under a preheated hot grill until the sugar bubbles and caramelises. Dust with cinnamon to serve.

Jimmy had steered clear of desserts during the competition but now the judges were impressed. "This is one of the best tasting dishes we've had all day. The flavour of the spices works beautifully with the creaminess."

Adam & Callum's **FINALE DISHES**

The Governor-General's dinner saw Claire determined not to cry over spilt milk, but lose her battle to french-trim a mountain of lamb cutlets. The Top 24 all returned for a light-hearted farewell Masterclass with George and Gary. Adam and Callum turned the tables on the judges with a final mystery box, and demonstrated some other skills they'd learnt from their MasterChef masters... "Hmmm, white chocolate and fish, George? Do you think that's a good combination? Is now the time to be trying something new?"

Now only the grand finalists remained: Adam and Callum. Who would be crowned Australia's next MasterChef? Together they'd cooked for and worked alongside some of the world's greatest chefs, created extraordinary dishes, and faced immense culinary challenges. Would the winner be the boy from the Barossa with a passion for desserts, or the brilliant lawyer with a creative flair for the exotic?

Three epic challenges now stood between them and the title: a basic skills test; an invention test to cook a core ingredient in three different ways; and a final pressure test.

In the invention test Callum displayed just how much he had learnt with this assiette of chicken and peas, turning ordinary ingredients into a dish that both looked and tasted utterly extraordinary.

"Gary, George, have you ever cooked with carrots before?" Callum and Adam have some fun with the professionals in the final Masterclass.

Callum's CHICKEN & PEA ASSIETTE

Serves **4**
Preparation **1 hour 45 minutes**
+ **3½ hours refrigeration**
Cooking **3½ hours**

Pea shoots and blanched fresh
   peas, to serve
PEA MOUSSE
2g gold-strength gelatine leaf
225g frozen peas, thawed
100ml pouring cream
CHICKEN STOCK
2 chicken carcasses*
1 onion, roughly chopped
1 carrot, roughly chopped
1 stalk celery, roughly chopped
4 cloves garlic, bruised
3 sprigs thyme
4 parsley stalks
8 black peppercorns
CONFIT CHICKEN WINGS
12 chicken wings

3 coriander seeds
4 black peppercorns
2 sprigs thyme
1 bay leaf
2½ tsp sea salt
600g duck fat (or 600ml
   olive oil)
2 tbs olive oil
BOUDIN BLANC
150g chicken breast fillet,
   roughly chopped
1 egg white
2 tsp pouring cream
VELOUTE SAUCE
2 tbs olive oil
2 eschalots, diced
½ carrot, diced

½ stalk celery, diced
2 cloves garlic, halved
3 sprigs thyme
1 bay leaf
80ml (⅓ cup) white wine
200ml pouring cream
SAUTEED CHICKEN OYSTERS
2 tbs olive oil
8 chicken oysters, skin on*
20g butter
SEARED SCALLOPS
2 tbs olive oil
20g butter
12 scallops, roe removed, cleaned

1 **To make pea mousse,** soak the gelatine leaf in cold water for 5 minutes to soften. Meanwhile, combine the peas, cream and 1 tbs water in a small saucepan and bring to the boil. Squeeze excess water from gelatine and add to pan; stir to dissolve. Transfer to a blender and blend for 1 minute or until smooth. Season with salt to taste. Pass through a fine sieve into a bowl over a bowl of ice and stir for 2 minutes or until cool. Cover with plastic wrap and refrigerate for 2 hours.

2 **To make chicken stock,** place all ingredients in a large saucepan and cover with 2L water. Bring almost to the boil, then reduce heat and simmer gently for 1½ hours, skimming frequently to remove any scum that rises to the surface. Strain stock through a chinois or a fine sieve lined with muslin.

3 **To make confit chicken wings**, locate the joints in the wing tips and opposite ends. Cut through joints between bones to remove tips and other ends so only middle wing sections remain.
  • Cut around skin 1cm from where wing tip was removed. Then cut between and around the 2 bones at the wing tip end to separate them for the first 2cm **(PIC 1)**. Separate the 2 bones at the other end of the wing with a small knick. Scrape down the meat of the 2 exposed bones to "french" them by removing the meat **(PIC 2)**. Use your fingers to twist out the larger bone **(PIC 3)** so 1 bone remains.
  • Push all the meat down to the non-frenched end of the bone. If the skin turns inside out during frenching, fold it back again. Use a knife to cut off the little knuckle at the end of the frenched bone. Repeat with remaining wings. Keep the leftover wing sections for the velouté sauce.

4 Pound the coriander seeds, black peppercorns, thyme and bay leaf with a mortar and pestle. Add the salt and pound a little. Rub the aromatic salt over the chicken wings. Refrigerate for 30 minutes. Preheat oven to 100°C. Melt the duck fat in a small ovenproof saucepan or roasting pan (or gently warm the olive oil, if using). Place the chicken wings into the duck fat or oil (it should not be sizzling, just producing the odd bubble). Cover with a round of baking paper and transfer to the oven. Cook for 90 minutes. Remove the wings with a slotted spoon, cover and refrigerate until needed.

5 To make boudin blanc, place chicken breast in a small food processor and add a pinch of salt. Process until chicken forms a ball, then add the egg white and blend again. Add the cream and pulse briefly – don't overmix or the cream will split. Layer 3 sheets of plastic wrap on top of each other.
   • Spoon the chicken onto the plastic in a line. Carefully roll up into a sausage 4cm in diameter, twist plastic at both ends and tie with kitchen string. Refrigerate for 1 hour, or until required.

6 To make velouté sauce, heat the olive oil in a large deep frying pan. Add the reserved wing pieces and cook over medium–high heat for 5 minutes or until starting to brown. Add the eschalots, carrot, celery and garlic and cook until golden brown. Add the thyme and bay leaf. Reheat 600ml of the stock (freeze the rest for another use).
   • Deglaze the pan with the wine. When the wine has almost completely reduced, add the hot stock and simmer until reduced by half. Strain into a clean pan, add the cream and simmer gently over low heat for 10 minutes. Season to taste. Cover and keep hot for serving.

7 Fill a deep frying pan with water and heat to 75°C on a kitchen thermometer. Add the boudin blanc and poach for 15 minutes, turning occasionally to ensure even cooking, or until pale and firm when gently squeezed. Remove from the water and cool slightly.

8 To cook sautéed chicken oysters, heat the oil in a small frying pan over medium–high heat. Season chicken oysters on the skin-side with salt. Cook, skin-side down, for 1½ minutes or until skin is crisp. Add the butter to the pan, turn chicken and cook, basting with butter, for 45 seconds or until cooked through. Keep warm.

9 To cook seared scallops, heat the oil and butter in a small frying pan. Season the scallops with salt. Cook over high heat for 1 minute, then turn and cook for 20 seconds. Keep warm.

10 To finish confit chicken wings, heat the olive oil in a large frying pan. Cook the wings over high heat for 1 minute on each side or until crisp.

11 To serve, unwrap the boudin blanc and trim ends. Cut into slices the same thickness as the scallops. Arrange scallops and boudin blanc on serving plates and arrange wings and oysters around. Add quenelles of pea mousse, pea shoots and fresh peas. Drizzle a little sauce around the plate.

CHICKEN CARCASS is the remains of the whole bird once the breasts and legs have been removed. Your butcher will supply them. **CHICKEN OYSTERS** are small pieces of dark meat on the back of the chicken, near the thighs. Ask your butcher. If you can't buy them separately, buy 8 chicken thigh cutlets. Starting from the top of the thigh along the backbone and heading to the tail end, carefully run your thumb between bone and flesh. You will quickly locate a small hollow in the thigh bone which contains the oyster. Ease it away and trim it off with the skin.

Adam's THREE LITTLE PIGS

Pork belly is Adam's favourite cut of meat. "It's incredibly versatile but has to be cooked correctly. Choosing it for the 'three ways' invention test was a bit of a risk (the judges thought I was crazy) but I didn't think the finale was a time to play safe." Adam minced and simmered the pork belly in custard, made a meltingly soft confit with a green salsa that Matt Moran wanted the recipe for, and double-steamed buns with red rum pork belly. "This is beauty on a plate. It's who you are, Adam. You are a brilliant cook," said George.

SIMMERED PORK IN STEAMED EGG CUSTARD

4 dried shiitake mushrooms
200g pork belly, skin removed,
   meat and fat minced
1 tsp preserved tofu*
2 tbs fish sauce
1 tbs cooking caramel

2 tbs sake
1 tbs mirin
1 tbs caster sugar
½ large onion, finely diced
1 clove garlic, minced
1 tsp Tianjin preserved vegetable*

3 tsp arrowroot
1 tsp dashi powder
2 eggs
1 tbs sake, extra
Ground white pepper and celery
   cress, to serve

1 Place the shiitake mushrooms in a heatproof bowl and cover with 250ml (1 cup) boiling water. Soak for 20 minutes or until soft. Discard the stalks and dice the caps. Reserve the soaking liquid. Meanwhile, combine the pork and tofu and leave for 30 minutes for the flavours to develop.

2 Mix the fish sauce, cooking caramel, sake, mirin and sugar in a small saucepan and add 150ml of the reserved mushroom liquid (there should be 2–3cm liquid in the pan). Add the onion and garlic and bring to the boil. Reduce the heat to low and simmer for 5 minutes.

3 Add the diced mushrooms, preserved vegetable and pork mixture to the pan and simmer for a further 7–10 minutes, breaking up the pork with a wooden spoon until cooked. Dilute the arrowroot in 2 tablespoons of the mushroom liquid and stir into the pan. Cook for 1 minute further until the mixture is thickened and glossy. Leave to cool slightly, then spoon into six 125ml (½-cup) ramekins. Refrigerate for 30 minutes or until cold.

4 Mix the dashi powder with 250ml (1 cup) water at room temperature. Break the eggs into a bowl and lift the white and yolks gently with chopsticks to break up the egg without aerating the mix. Add the dashi broth and extra sake and stir without whisking until combined. Pass through a fine sieve to ensure the mixture is smooth but do not incorporate any air bubbles.

5 Pour the egg mixture on top of the pork and place the ramekins into a large steamer. Place over a pan of boiling water and cook over medium heat for 15–20 minutes or until the custard is set. Garnish with ground white pepper and celery cress.

PRESERVED TOFU can be found on the shelf (not refrigerated) in good Asian grocers. **TIANJIN PRESERVED VEGETABLE** (often cabbage or radish) is found in good Asian grocers in sealed packs or earthenware jars.

Adam's **THREE LITTLE PIGS**

CONFIT PORK BELLY & SCALLOPS
WITH PORK CRACKLING & CHILLI CORIANDER SALSA

2 cloves garlic
2 tsp white pepper
220g pork belly, with skin
500ml (2 cups) olive oil
Vegetable oil, to deep-fry

2 tbs olive oil, extra
6 scallops
CHILLI CORIANDER SALSA
1 large green chilli, seeded
⅓ cup finely chopped coriander

2 tsp caster sugar
1 tbs fish sauce
2 tbs rice wine vinegar
1 tbs tamari

1 **To make confit pork belly,** preheat oven to 110°C. Pound the garlic, white pepper and ½ tsp salt to a smooth paste, using a mortar and pestle. Remove the skin from the pork and reserve. Cut the meat into 1cm batons. Rub the paste all over the pork batons and marinate for at least 15 minutes.

2 Put the pork in a small deep roasting pan or ovenproof saucepan. Pour in enough olive oil to completely submerge the pork. Cover with a piece of baking paper and cook in the oven for 1 hour.

3 Meanwhile, rub the pork skin liberally with 1 tsp salt and place into a dehydrator for at least 1 hour.* Fill a deep-fryer or large saucepan one-third full with vegetable oil and heat over medium heat to 180°C (or until a cube of bread turns golden in 10 seconds). Brush excess salt from pork skin and fry for 2–3 minutes or until well coloured. Drain on paper towel. The skin will become crisp on cooling. Break or chop into 1cm pieces.

4 **To make chilli coriander salsa,** finely chop the chilli and coriander together until well combined. Stir together the sugar, fish sauce, vinegar and tamari until sugar has dissolved. Add the chilli and coriander. Mix well and leave for at least 5 minutes for flavours to develop.

5 Heat the extra olive oil in a frying pan over medium–high heat. Sear the scallops for 1 minute on each side or until just cooked through. Cut in half horizontally.

6 Remove the confit pork from the oil with a slotted spoon. Place a small mound onto each plate, top with the scallop halves and scatter with crackling. Spoon the chilli coriander salsa around the pork.

IF YOU DON'T have a dehydrator, leave the salt-rubbed pork skin uncovered in the fridge overnight.

RED RUM BELLY BUNS WITH PICKLED CHILLI

220g lean pork belly, with skin
Vegetable oil, to deep-fry
250ml (1 cup) dashi broth
2 tbs dark rum
2 tbs sake
2 tbs cooking caramel (Karamel masakan)*
2 tbs soy sauce
1 tbs fish sauce
75g (1/3 cup) caster sugar

1/2 onion, diced
2 cloves garlic, chopped
2 star anise
1 cinnamon quill
1/2 vanilla bean, seeds scraped
Chopped chives, to serve
PICKLED CHILLI
1/4 cup (60ml) rice wine vinegar
1 tbs caster sugar
1 tsp salt

1 long red chilli, thinly sliced
LEMON PASTE
1 lemon
BUNS
1 tsp dry yeast
150g (1 cup) plain flour
1 1/2 tbs caster sugar
1/4 tsp baking powder
1 tbs vegetable oil

1 **To make lemon paste,** pour 2cm water into a pressure cooker. Wash the lemon well and place in the pressure cooker. Seal and heat over high heat until there is a constant hissing and steam is escaping. Reduce heat to medium or low following instructions to maintain medium–high pressure. Cook lemon for 15 minutes. Release steam according to manufacturer's instructions. Carefully remove lemon with a slotted spoon and cool slightly; discard any excess liquid. Cut lemon in half, remove the seeds and then purée the skin and pulp until smooth. Pass through a fine sieve and set aside.

2 **To make pickled chilli,** combine the vinegar, sugar and salt in a small saucepan. Stir over low–medium heat to dissolve the sugar, then increase the heat and bring to the boil. Remove from heat and add the chilli. Leave to cool completely, then drain.

3 Meanwhile, fill a saucepan with water and bring to a rapid boil. Add the pork belly and cook for 10 minutes. Drain, then pat dry with paper towel. Fill a deep-fryer or large saucepan one-third full with vegetable oil and heat over medium heat to 160°C (or until a cube of bread turns golden in 12 seconds). Fry the pork for 5 minutes or until well coloured.

4 Combine the dashi broth, rum, sake, caramel, soy sauce, fish sauce, caster sugar, onion, garlic, star anise, cinnamon and vanilla seeds in a saucepan. Stir over medium heat to dissolve the sugar, then bring to the boil. Pour 1.5cm water into a pressure cooker and fit the steamer tray or a trivet. Place a Pyrex bowl on the steamer tray and add the pork. Pour the boiling dashi mixture over the pork and add enough water to cover it completely. Place a round of baking paper over the pork. Cook for 1 hour, maintaining medium–high pressure as before. Remove the pork and slice thickly. Transfer the liquid to a deep frying pan and cook over high heat for 8 minutes or until reduced by half. Adjust the seasoning, then add the pork slices to warm through and coat with the sauce.

5 **To make the buns,** combine the yeast and 75ml lukewarm water in a bowl. Leave in a warm place for 10 minutes or until frothy. Sift the dry ingredients into a bowl and make a well in the centre. Add the yeast mixture and oil and stir with a wooden spoon until a dough starts to form. Oil your hands and gather the dough together. Knead for 10 minutes until smooth. Place in an oiled bowl, cover with a clean tea towel and leave in a warm place for 45 minutes or until doubled in size.

6 Knock down the dough with one punch. Cut into 4 portions and roll each piece into 3cm-diameter logs. Break off 3cm portions of dough and roll into balls (dough should make 16 balls).
   • Place balls about 3cm apart in 2 large bamboo steamers lined with baking paper. Leave in a warm place for 30 minutes or until well risen. Steam buns over simmering water for 8–10 minutes or until well risen, shiny and springy to touch.

7 Serve buns, lemon paste and pickled chilli topped with pork and a little sauce. Sprinkle with chives.

COOKING CARAMEL is available from Asian grocers.

Peter Gilmore

Peter Gilmore is executive chef of Australia's highest ranked restaurant in the world, Quay, in Sydney. Quay has been named Restaurant of the Year 2010 and 2009 by the *Sydney Morning Herald Good Food Guide*. It was only to be expected that Peter's finale pressure test dish would be something special.

In Peter's opinion, the key to success with this particular dish would be "organisation and concentration". **Guava and custard apple snow egg** is one of Peter's signature desserts. The "snow egg" is a sphere of poached meringue filled with custard apple ice-cream. But the "tricky part" of the recipe is the maltose tuile melted over the meringue with a blowtorch. "It knocks my socks off," said Adam in admiration. "Delicious doesn't come close to doing it justice."

"This is the hardest dish we've had on this show. This is a masterpiece... a three-hat wonder." Adam and Callum try not to be intimidated by Peter Gilmore's extraordinary snow egg.

Serves **6**
Preparation **3 hours**
+ 3 hours freezing
Cooking **1½ hours**

GUAVA & CUSTARD APPLE SNOW EGGS

Icing sugar, to dust
CUSTARD APPLE ICE-CREAM
100ml milk
3 egg yolks
100g caster sugar
3 soft ripe custard apples
  (450g each)
50ml pouring cream
GUAVA GRANITA
100g caster sugar
400g (about 3) strawberry
  guavas, peeled, seeded,
  roughly chopped

100g strawberries,
  hulled, halved
VANILLA CUSTARD
400ml pouring cream
1 vanilla bean, split, seeds
  scraped
1 egg
3 egg yolks
80g caster sugar
POACHED MERINGUE
150g (about 3) egg whites
150g caster sugar
canola oil spray

GUAVA FOOL
175g caster sugar
½ vanilla bean, seeds scraped
400g (about 3) strawberry
  guavas, peeled, seeded,
  roughly chopped
200ml double cream
MALTOSE TUILES
100ml caster sugar
250ml (1 cup) maltose syrup*
25g flaked almonds

1 To make custard apple ice-cream, place milk in a small saucepan and bring almost to the boil. Whisk egg yolks and sugar in a bowl until combined. Whisking continuously, gradually add milk to egg yolk mixture. Return mixture to pan over low heat and, using a wooden spoon, stir continuously without boiling until thick enough to coat the back of the spoon. Place pan over a bowl of ice and whisk for 3 minutes to cool rapidly. Leave to cool completely.

• Meanwhile, line a sieve with muslin and place over a bowl. Scoop flesh from custard apples into the lined sieve. Gather cloth at the top and squeeze tightly to obtain a clear juice. Whisk 150ml juice into the cooled custard with the cream, then churn in an ice-cream maker following the manufacturer's instructions. Transfer to an airtight container and freeze for at least 3 hours or until needed.

2 To make guava granita, place sugar and 500ml (2 cups) water in a saucepan and bring to the boil, stirring to dissolve sugar. Reduce heat to medium, add guavas and strawberries and simmer for 10 minutes. Remove from the heat and leave for 30 minutes for flavours to infuse.

• Strain through a fine sieve into an 11 x 22cm loaf tin or other small container, discarding solids. Freeze, scraping with a fork every hour to break up ice crystals, for 3 hours or until frozen in flakes.

3 To make vanilla custard, preheat oven to 150°C. Place cream, vanilla bean and seeds in a small saucepan and bring almost to the boil. Whisk egg, yolks and sugar in a bowl. Whisking continuously, gradually add cream mixture to egg mixture. Discard the vanilla bean.

• Pour into six 125ml (½-cup) ramekins or moulds. Place ramekins in a roasting pan and pour boiling water into pan to reach one-third of the way up side of ramekins **(PIC 1)**. Bake for 25 minutes or until custards are just set. Refrigerate custards for 1½ hours to chill. (These will become guava fool later.)

4 To make poached meringue, preheat oven to 150°C. Using an electric mixer, whisk egg whites to soft peaks, then gradually add sugar and whisk until stiff peaks form and sugar is dissolved. Spray 12 hemisphere moulds* lightly with canola oil spray. Spoon meringue into a piping bag fitted with a 1cm nozzle and pipe into moulds, mounding the meringue above the mould.

- Place moulds in a roasting pan and pour 3cm boiling water into pan. Bake for 15 minutes or until just set and slightly browned. Cool for 2 minutes.
- Use a wet knife to trim off tops of meringues flush with tops of hemisphere moulds. Gently un-mould meringues and place, cut-side up, on a tray lined with baking paper. Refrigerate until needed. Increase oven temperature to 180°C.

5 **To make guava fool,** combine sugar, 250ml (1 cup) water, vanilla bean and seeds in a saucepan and bring to the boil. Reduce heat to medium, add guavas and simmer for 10 minutes or until tender.
- Using a slotted spoon, remove guavas and process with 80ml (⅓ cup) syrup in a food processor, adding a little more syrup if necessary, to form a thick purée. Strain through a fine sieve and transfer mixture to an airtight container. Refrigerate until needed.

6 **To make maltose tuiles,** place sugar, maltose and 125ml (½ cup) water in a small saucepan and stir over low-medium heat until sugar dissolves. Brush down the side of the pan with a wet pastry brush to prevent sugar crystals forming. Cook until syrup forms a golden caramel. Immediately add almonds, swirling pan to coat almonds in caramel, then pour onto an oven tray lined with baking paper. Set aside until praline is hard and cool.

7 **To cook maltose tuiles,** preheat oven to 180°C. Put praline in a food processor and process to a fine powder. Cut six 11cm-round holes in a piece of cardboard or acetate. Place template on an oven tray lined with baking paper. Place half the ground praline in a sieve and sift over the holes. Lift away the template **(PIC 2)** and tip excess mixture back into sieve.
- Bake for 4 minutes or until tuile mixture melts to form thin biscuits. Cool tuiles for 1 minute, then carefully peel off the baking paper. Repeat to make another 6 tuiles (you only need 6, but there may be breakages). Store any leftover mixture in an airtight container for another time.

8 **To make guava fool,** scoop custard from 3 ramekins into a bowl. (The remaining 3 custards are not needed, so serve separately.) Add cream to bowl and whisk to soft peaks. Refrigerate until needed. Add guava purée and, using a large spoon, fold in until partially mixed to create a ripple effect.

9 **To assemble,** using a melon baller or teaspoon measure, take a small scoop from the centre of each hemisphere meringue, taking care not to break through the outer edge. Fill the holes on 6 meringues with a heaped teaspoonful of custard apple ice-cream **(PIC 3)**. Sandwich with the remaining 6 meringues to make complete spheres – use wet fingers to gently stick the 2 halves together.
- Place a tuile on top of each sphere. Using a kitchen blowtorch around the edge of the tuile, gently melt so that the tuile collapses, taking on the shape of the sphere, patting it down if necessary. Dust the spheres liberally with icing sugar.
- Spoon the guava fool into wide glasses and top with spoonfuls of granita. Using 2 teaspoons, lower a snow egg into each glass and serve immediately.

MALTOSE SYRUP is a thick sweet malt syrup available from Asian grocers. **HEMISPHERE MOULDS** are from Chef's Warehouse. You'll need to cut down a 28-hole 6cm silicone hemisphere mould tray.

Cooking Notes

Blanch To blanch a food is to very briefly par-cook it. For example, green vegetables such as beans or asparagus can be dropped into boiling water, cooked or left to stand for 1–2 minutes, then drained and immediately dropped into iced water to stop the cooking process. This preserves their colour and texture, while taking away the raw flavour.

Blind bake To precook a pastry shell before filling. Line the uncooked pastry with baking paper, extending it well over the sides. Fill with dried beans, uncooked rice or baking weights. Cook for the time instructed, then remove the paper and weights and cook again, as instructed, until the pastry is golden and cooked. When blind baking pastry, you may be instructed to dock it. This simply means to prick the base with a fork to prevent air pockets forming under the pastry during cooking.

Caramelisation The process of cooking sugar until it turns liquid and golden. This also refers to achieving a desirable brown colour on foods, giving a good indication of flavour development.

Cartouche A paper lid that is placed directly onto the surface of food to slow down the evaporation of moisture during cooking. To make a round cartouche, take a square sheet of baking paper slightly larger than your pan and fold it in half diagonally. Fold twice more to make a thin triangle. Holding the point of the triangle in the centre of the pan to gauge the size, trim the outer edge on a curve where it reaches the side of the pan. Unfold and place onto the food.

Chinois A cone-shaped, fine-mesh sieve. The shape allows liquid to run through more quickly than in a round-bottomed sieve.

Confit Originally a method of preservation, a confit is food (for example, meat or poultry cuts) cooked gently in a fat. The food is then cooled and stored in that fat. Fruit and vegetables can also be prepared to make a confit in sugar syrup or oil. A confit is tender and flavoursome and is now often used as a cooking method rather than a means to preserve and store foods.

Deglaze To add liquid such as wine, stock or vinegar to a pan after cooking meat or vegetables. The liquid lifts any caramelised particles from the pan, adding to the flavour of the finished dish or sauce.

French To french meat is to scrape the bone clean of meat and sinew for presentation. Lamb racks or cutlets are often prepared in this way. You can french bones yourself or ask your butcher to do it for you.

Gelatine Comes in sheet or powdered form. Professionals will choose the sheets as they have a neutral taste, give clear jellies a beautiful appearance and are less likely to cause problems during preparation. They are available from specialist food shops and some delis. Use the weight and strength asked for in the recipe (i.e. gold- or titanium-strength).

Ginger Unless 'ground ginger' is required, ginger is fresh and should be peeled before use. It is usually required to be grated or finely chopped.

Grinding & crushing Spices are often roasted and ground before use. If you don't have a mortar and pestle, use a food processor for grinding. Alternatively, seal spices in a sandwich bag and crush by hitting with a rolling pin or the flat side of a meat mallet.

Julienne To cut into julienne is to cut a food (usually a vegetable) into uniform matchstick-shaped pieces.

Knock down A recipe will often say to 'knock down' dough after proving. This is done by a simple punch, which releases accumulated gases in the dough.

Mandolin A kitchen implement used to cut very thin, uniform slices, usually from vegetables. A mandolin may come with other blades to give different slicing effects, such as julienned, rippled or waffled.

Micro cress, herbs or greens

Used as a garnish, these are very small plants, usually harvested when the first two leaves appear. You can buy them in punnets from good greengrocers and nurseries. Use scissors to snip the stems, rather than pulling them out of the growing medium.

Non-reactive

When marinating foods, always use a dish made from a non-reactive material, such as glass or ceramic, which will not be affected by any acidic ingredients in the marinade (wine, vinegar or citrus juice). Stainless-steel bowls are fine for use, but other metals can cause an unpleasant flavour to develop in the food.

Onions

You will find several different varieties referred to:
• Onions are the brown variety
• Red onions
• Spring onions are the long, thin green variety
• Bulb spring onions are long, thin and green with a white bulb at the end
• Eschalots are the small sweet variety with golden-coloured skin, also called French shallots
• Asian red eschalots are the small sweet variety with pink-red skin, available from Asian grocers.

Pastry

When making pastry, butter is rubbed into flour until the mixture resembles coarse breadcrumbs. Only use your fingertips, as they are cooler than the rest of your hands. If you like, this can be done in a food processor, then any liquid (such as water or egg) added and pulsed in short bursts until the mixture forms moist clumps. The dough is then turned out, gathered together and rolled out as required. Always take care not to over-handle pastry: this causes shrinkage and a tough texture.

Pin bone

To remove small bones from fish. When preparing a side of salmon, for example, run your fingers along the top of the flesh from the tail end to the front to feel for these tiny bones. Remove them with tweezers.

Preparing prawns

First remove the head. Peel off the shell with the legs and, if removing the tail, squeeze it and pull gently from the body. To remove the digestive tract, using a sharp knife, score down the back to expose the dark 'vein' and pull it out (this is known as 'deveining'). To remove without cutting the prawn, carefully pull out from the head end.

Quenelle

Refers to an oval shape, usually used for presentation of cream, ice-cream or mousse. To make quenelles, use two spoons that have been dipped in hot water. Scoop up some of the mixture in one spoon, then transfer gently from spoon to spoon to form a neat oval shape.

Seasoning

Unless stated otherwise, to season means to add salt and freshly ground black pepper to taste.

Temperatures

• All oven temperatures are for conventional, non-fan-forced ovens. If you are using a fan-forced oven, set the temperature to 20°C lower than that stated in the recipe.
• Use a cooking thermometer to measure the temperature of oil when deep-frying. These thermometers are used for accuracy when making sugar syrups and other types of toffee work. You can also use them to ensure the correct temperature for poaching and when making confit.
• When cooking large cuts of meat such as lamb rumps or beef fillets, use a meat thermometer to measure the internal temperature of the meat to avoid under- or over-cooking.

Weights & sizes

• For accuracy, it is always better to weigh ingredients rather than use cup measures, particularly when baking.
• 1 tablespoon (tbs) holds 20ml or 4 teaspoons (tsp).
• Fruits and vegetables are medium-sized unless specified.
• Unless specified, all eggs used are 59g (extra large).

Zest

Finely grated (unless otherwise specified) rind of citrus. Wash fruit well before grating and avoid the bitter white pith just below the rind. Zest contains highly aromatic oils that give flavour and fragrance to foods.

Index

HarperCollins*Publishers*

First published in Australia in 2010 by HarperCollins*Publishers* Australia Pty Limited
ABN 36 009 913 517 harpercollins.com.au
25 Ryde Road, Pymble, Sydney, NSW 2073, Australia
31 View Road, Glenfield, Auckland 0627, New Zealand

National Library of Australia Cataloguing-in-Publication data:
Masterchef. Volume 2.
ISBN 978 0 7322 9186 0 (pbk.)
Includes index. Masterchef (Television program). Cooking, Australian.
641.5994

Editor-in-chief: **Trudi Jenkins**
Creative director: **Scott Cassidy**
Food director: **Sophia Young**

Project editor and writer: **Jane Price**
Project designer and art director:
  Annette Fitzgerald
Project food editor: **Tracy Rutherford**
Food photography: **Jeremy Simons**
Additional food photography: **Steve Brown,**
  Ben Dearnley, Rob Palmer, Brett Stevens

Stylist: **Kristine Duran-Thiessen**
Stylist's assistant: **Erica Vercueil**
Additional styling: **Julz Beresford,**
  Yael Grinham, Amber Keller,
  Berni Smithies
Food preparation: **Julie Ballard**
Food preparation assistants: **Andrew Ballard,**
  Daniel Taplin
Series photography: **Stuart Bryce**
Additional series photography: **Jodie Hutchinson,**
  Nigel Wright

Stephanie Alexander's Duck Dinner (page 144) reprinted from *The Cook's Companion* (Penguin) with permission from Stephanie Alexander
All meat supplied by Hudson Meats (hudsonmeats.com.au)
All fruit and vegetables supplied by Velluti's (vellutis.com.au)

The publisher wishes to thank the following for their generosity in supplying props and kitchenware for this book: Aeria Country Floors (aeria.com.au); Bison Australia (bisonhome.com); Citta Design (cittadesign.com); Clay & Flax (clayandflax.com.au); Deb Taylor at Little White Dish (littlewhitedish.com.au); Ecology Home (03) 9765 5700; Everdure Kitchen (everdurekitchen.com.au); Georg Jensen (georgjensenstore.com.au); Ikea (ikea.com.au); VGM International (vgmimports.com.au); Laminex Australia (laminex.com.au); LSA International (lsainternational.com); Milk & Sugar (milkandsugar.com.au); Robert Gordon (robertgordanaustralia.com); Royal Doulton (royaldoulton.com.au); Studio William (studiowilliam.com); Tablekraft (tablekraft.com.au); TefalMasterchef (tefalmasterchef.com); Thonet (thonet.com.au); Villeroy & Boch (villeroy-boch.com); Waterford Wedgwood (waterfordwedgwood.com.au); White Home (whitehome.com.au)

Cover design by **Priscilla Nielsen**. Back cover images by **Stuart Bryce**

Colour reproduction by Graphic Print Group, Adelaide.
Printed and bound in China by RR Donnelley on 128gsm matt art